Workshop on the Future of Language Modeling for HLT 2012

Will We Ever Really Replace the N-gram Model?

Held at the 2012 Conference of the North American Chapter of the Association for Computational Linguistics: Human Language Technologies (NAACL-HLT 2012)

Montreal, Quebec, Canada
3 – 8 June 2012

ISBN: 978-1-62276-573-7

Printed from e-media with permission by:

Curran Associates, Inc.
57 Morehouse Lane
Red Hook, NY 12571

Some format issues inherent in the e-media version may also appear in this print version.

Printed by Curran Associates, Inc. (2013)

For permission requests, please contact the Association for Computational Linguistics at the address below.

Association for Computational Linguistics
209 N. Eighth Street
Stroudsburg, Pennsylvania 18360

Phone: 1-570-476-8006
Fax: 1-570-476-0860

acl@aclweb.org

Additional copies of this publication are available from:

Curran Associates, Inc.
57 Morehouse Lane
Red Hook, NY 12571 USA
Phone: 845-758-0400
Fax: 845-758-2634
Email: curran@proceedings.com
Web: www.proceedings.com

Introduction

Welcome to the NAACL-HLT workshop: Will We Ever Really Replace the N-gram Model? On the Future of Language Modeling for HLT!

Language models are a critical component in many speech and natural language processing technologies, such as speech recognition and understanding, voice search, conversational interaction and machine translation. Over the last few decades, several advanced language modeling ideas have been proposed. Some of these approaches have focused on incorporating linguistic information such as syntax and semantics whereas others have focused on fundamental modeling and parameter estimation techniques. Although tremendous progress has been made in language modeling, n-grams are still very much the state-of-the-art due to the simplicity of the model and good performance they can achieve.

The aim of this workshop is to bring together researchers from natural language processing, linguistics and spoken language processing and to provide a venue to explore and discuss new approaches to language modeling for different applications. We have received an excellent set of papers focused on neural network language models, discriminative language models and language models using explicit syntactic information. Some of the papers investigated these models with different architectures, while others used large scale and unsupervised set-ups.

Our workshop will feature two keynote talks. We begin with a keynote from Shankar Kumar (Google Inc.) and will conclude with the second keynote from Brian Roark (Oregon Health and Science University). We will close with an open discussion led by several prominent researchers that will summarize the emerging areas of research in language modeling, the issues and challenges for various tasks that we have learnt/highlighted over the course of this workshop, common resources and evaluation challenges that can be posed to the research community.

With the advent of smart phone technologies and increased use of natural language interactions for many day-to-day tasks, it is the correct time to bring together experts in the fields of linguistics, speech and natural language processing and machine learning from industry and academia to share their ideas and set the stage for the future of language modeling.

We are especially grateful to the program committee for their hard work and the presenters for their excellent papers.

Organizing Committee

Bhuvana Ramabhadran, Sanjeev Khudanpur and Ebru Arisoy

Organizers:

Bhuvana Ramabhadran, IBM T.J. Watson Research Center (USA)
Sanjeev Khudanpur, Johns Hopkins University (USA)
Ebru Arisoy, IBM T.J. Watson Research Center (USA)

Program Committee:

Ciprian Chelba, Google Inc. (USA)
Stanley F. Chen, IBM T.J. Watson Research Center (USA)
Ahmad Emami, IBM T.J. Watson Research Center (USA)
Tomas Mikolov, Brno University of Technology (USA)
Hermann Ney, RWTH Aachen University (Germany)
Patrick Nguyen, Google Inc. (USA)
Kemal Oflazer, Carnegie Mellon University (Qatar)
Brian Roark, Oregon Health and Science University (USA)
Murat Saraclar, Bogazici University (Turkey)
Holger Schwenk, University of LIUM (France)
Peng Xu, Google Inc. (USA)
Geoffrey Zweig, Microsoft (USA)

Invited Speakers:

Shankar Kumar, Google Inc. (USA)
Brian Roark, Oregon Health and Science University (USA)

Table of Contents

Workshop Program

Friday, June 8, 2012

9:15-9:30 Opening Remarks

9:30-10:30 Invited Talk

10:30-11:00 Coffee Break

\+ Morning Session

11:00–11:25 *Measuring the Influence of Long Range Dependencies with Neural Network Language Models*
Hai-Son Le, Alexandre Allauzen and François Yvon

11:25–11:50 *Large, Pruned or Continuous Space Language Models on a GPU for Statistical Machine Translation*
Holger Schwenk, Anthony Rousseau and Mohammed Attik

11:50–12:15 *Deep Neural Network Language Models*
Ebru Arisoy, Tara N. Sainath, Brian Kingsbury and Bhuvana Ramabhadran

12:15-14:00 Lunch

\+ Afternoon Session

14:00–14:25 *A Challenge Set for Advancing Language Modeling*
Geoffrey Zweig and Chris J.C. Burges

14:25–14:50 *Unsupervised Vocabulary Adaptation for Morph-based Language Models*
André Mansikkaniemi and Mikko Kurimo

14:50–15:15 *Large-scale discriminative language model reranking for voice-search*
Preethi Jyothi, Leif Johnson, Ciprian Chelba and Brian Strope

15:15–15:40 *Revisiting the Case for Explicit Syntactic Information in Language Models*
Ariya Rastrow, Sanjeev Khudanpur and Mark Dredze

15:40-16:00 Coffee Break

Friday, June 8, 2012 (continued)

16:00-17:00 Invited Talk

17:00-18:00 Closing Remarks

Measuring the Influence of Long Range Dependencies with Neural Network Language Models

Le Hai Son and **Alexandre Allauzen** and **François Yvon**
Univ. Paris-Sud and LIMSI/CNRS
rue John von Neumann, 91 403 Orsay cedex, France
Firstname.Lastname@limsi.fr

Abstract

In spite of their well known limitations, most notably their use of very local contexts, n-gram language models remain an essential component of many Natural Language Processing applications, such as Automatic Speech Recognition or Statistical Machine Translation. This paper investigates the potential of language models using larger context windows comprising up to the 9 previous words. This study is made possible by the development of several novel Neural Network Language Model architectures, which can easily fare with such large context windows. We experimentally observed that extending the context size yields clear gains in terms of perplexity and that the n-gram assumption is statistically reasonable as long as n is sufficiently high, and that efforts should be focused on improving the estimation procedures for such large models.

1 Introduction

Conventional n-gram Language Models (LMs) are a cornerstone of modern language modeling for Natural Language Processing (NLP) systems such as statistical machine translation (SMT) and Automatic Speech Recognition (ASR). After more than two decades of experimenting with these models in a variety of languages, genres, datasets and applications, the vexing conclusion is that these models are very difficult to improve upon. Many variants of the simple n-gram model have been discussed in the literature; yet, very few of these variants have shown to deliver consistent performance gains. Among these, smoothing techniques, such as Good-Turing, Witten-Bell and Kneser-Ney smoothing schemes (see (Chen and Goodman, 1996) for an empirical overview and (Teh, 2006) for a Bayesian interpretation) are used to compute estimates for the probability of unseen events, which are needed to achieve state-of-the-art performance in large-scale settings. This is because, even when using the simplifying n-gram assumption, maximum likelihood estimates remain unreliable and tend to overerestimate the probability of those rare n-grams that are actually observed, while the remaining lots receive a too small (null) probability.

One of the most successful alternative to date is to use *distributed word representations* (Bengio et al., 2003) to estimate the n-gram models. In this approach, the discrete representation of the vocabulary, where each word is associated with an arbitrary index, is replaced with a continuous representation, where words that are distributionally similar are represented as neighbors. This turns n-gram distributions into smooth functions of the word representation. These representations and the associated estimates are jointly computed using a multi-layer neural network architecture. The use of neural-networks language models was originally introduced in (Bengio et al., 2003) and successfully applied to large-scale speech recognition (Schwenk and Gauvain, 2002; Schwenk, 2007) and machine translation tasks (Allauzen et al., 2011). Following these initial successes, the neural approach has recently been extended in several promising ways (Mikolov et al., 2011a; Kuo et al., 2010; Liu et al., 2011).

Another difference between conventional and

neural network language models (NNLMs) that has often been overlooked is the ability of the latter to fare with extended contexts (Schwenk and Koehn, 2008; Emami et al., 2008); in comparison, standard n-gram LMs rarely use values of n above $n = 4$ or 5, mainly because of data sparsity issues and the lack of generalization of the standard estimates, notwithstanding the complexity of the computations incurred by the smoothing procedures (see however (Brants et al., 2007) for an attempt to build very large models with a simple smoothing scheme).

The recent attempts of Mikolov et al. (2011b) to resuscitate recurrent neural network architectures goes one step further in that direction, as a recurrent network simulates an unbounded history size, whereby the memory of all the previous words accumulates in the form of activation patterns on the hidden layer. Significant improvements in ASR using these models were reported in (Mikolov et al., 2011b; Mikolov et al., 2011a). It must however be emphasized that the use of a recurrent structure implies an increased complexity of the training and inference procedures, as compared to a standard feed-forward network. This means that this approach cannot handle large training corpora as easily as n-gram models, which makes it difficult to perform a fair comparison between these two architectures and to assess the real benefits of using very large contexts.

The contribution is this paper is two-fold. We first analyze the results of various NNLMs to assess whether long range dependencies are efficient in language modeling, considering history sizes ranging from 3 words to an unbounded number of words (recurrent architecture). A by-product of this study is a slightly modified version of n-gram SOUL model (Le et al., 2011a) that aims at quantitatively estimating the influence of context words both in terms of their position and their part-of-speech information. The experimental set-up is based on a large scale machine translation task. We then propose a head to head comparison between the feed-forward and recurrent NNLMs. To make this comparison fair, we introduce an extension of the SOUL model that approximates the recurrent architecture with a limited history. While this extension achieves performance that are similar to the recurrent model on small datasets, the associated training procedure can benefit from all the speed-ups and tricks of standard feedforward NNLM (mini-batch and resampling), which make it able to handle large training corpora. Furthermore, we show that this approximation can also be effectively used to bootstrap the training of a "true" recurrent architecture.

The rest of this paper is organized as follows. We first recollect, in Section 2, the basics of NNLMs architectures. We then describe, in Section 3, a number of ways to speed up training for our "pseudo-recurrent" model. We finally report, in Section 4, various experimental results aimed at measuring the impact of large contexts, first in terms of perplexity, then on a realistic English to French translation task.

2 Language modeling in a continuous space

Let $\mathcal{V}$ be a finite vocabulary, language models define distributions over sequences[1] of tokens (typically words) w_1^L in $\mathcal{V}^+$ as follows:

$$P(w_1^L) = \prod_{i=1}^{L} P(w_i|w_1^{i-1}) \tag{1}$$

Modeling the joint distribution of several discrete random variables (such as words in a sentence) is difficult, especially in NLP applications where $\mathcal{V}$ typically contains hundreds of thousands words. In the n-gram model, the context is limited to the $n-1$ previous words, yielding the following factorization:

$$P(w_1^L) = \prod_{i=1}^{L} P(w_i|w_{i-n+1}^{i-1}) \tag{2}$$

Neural network language models (Bengio et al., 2003) propose to represent words in a continuous space and to estimate the probability distribution as a smooth function of this representation. Figure 1 provides an overview of this approach. The context words are first projected in a continuous space using the shared matrix $\mathbf{R}$. Denoting $\mathbf{v}$ the 1-of-V coding vector of word v (all null except for the vth component which is set to 1), its projection vector is the vth line of $\mathbf{R}$: $\mathbf{R}^T\mathbf{v}$. The hidden layer $\mathbf{h}$ is then computed as a non-linear function of these vectors. Finally, the probability of all possible outcomes are computed using one or several softmax layer(s).

[1] w_i^j denotes a sequence of tokens $w_i \dots j$ when $j \geq i$, or the empty sequence otherwise.

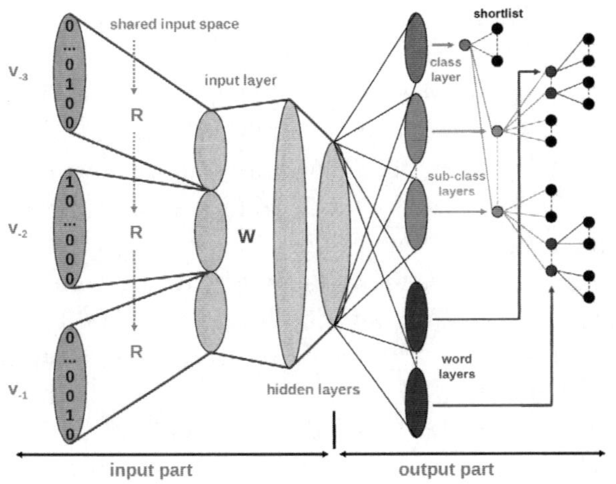

Figure 1: 4-*gram model with SOUL at the output layer.*

This architecture can be divided in two parts, with the hidden layer in the middle: the input part (on the left hand side of the graph) which aims at representing the context of the prediction; and the output part (on the right hand side) which computes the probability of all possible successor words given the context. In the remaining of this section, we describe these two parts in more detail.

2.1 Input Layer Structure

The input part computes a continuous representation of the context in the form of a context vector $\mathbf{h}$ to be processed through the hidden layer.

2.1.1 N-gram Input Layer

Using the standard n-gram assumption of equation (2), the context is made up of the sole $n-1$ previous words. In a n-gram NNLM, these words are projected in the shared continuous space and their representations are then concatenated to form a single vector $\mathbf{i}$, as illustrated in the left part of Figure 1:

$$\mathbf{i} = \{\mathbf{R}^T\mathbf{v}_{-(n-1)}; \mathbf{R}^T\mathbf{v}_{-(n-2)}; \ldots; \mathbf{R}^T\mathbf{v}_{-1}\}, \quad (3)$$

where $\mathbf{v}_{-k}$ is the kth previous word. A non-linear transformation is then applied to compute the first hidden layer $\mathbf{h}$ as follows:

$$\mathbf{h} = \operatorname{sigm}(\mathbf{W}\mathbf{i} + \mathbf{b}), \quad (4)$$

with sigm the sigmoid function. This kind of architecture will be referred to as a feed-forward NNLM.

Conventional n-gram LMs are usually limited to small values of n, and using n greater that 4 or 5 does not seem to be of much use. Indeed, previous experiments using very large speech recognition systems indicated that the gain obtained by increasing the n-gram order from 4 to 5 is almost negligible, whereas the model size increases drastically. While using large context seems to be very impractical with back-off LMs, the situation is quite different for NNLMs due to their specific architecture. In fact, increasing the context length for a NNLM mainly implies to expend the projection layer with one supplementary projection vector, which can furthermore be computed very easily through a simple look-up operation. The overall complexity of NNLMs thus only grows linearly with n in the worst case (Schwenk, 2007).

In order to better investigate the impact of each context position in the prediction, we introduce a slight modification of this architecture in a manner analog to the proposal of Collobert and Weston (2008). In this variation, the computation of the hidden layer defined by equation (4) is replaced by:

$$\mathbf{h} = \operatorname{sigm}\left(\max_k \left[\mathbf{W_k}\mathbf{R}^T\mathbf{v}_{-k}\right] + \mathbf{b}\right), \quad (5)$$

where $\mathbf{W_k}$ is the sub-matrix of $\mathbf{W}$ comprising the columns related to the kth history word, and the max is to be understood component-wise. The product $\mathbf{W_k}\mathbf{R}^T$ can then be considered as defining the projection matrix for the kth position. After the projection of all the context words, the max function selects, for each dimension l, among the $n-1$ values $([\mathbf{W_k}\mathbf{R}^T\mathbf{v}_{-k}]_l)$ the most active one, which we also assume to be the most relevant for the prediction.

2.1.2 Recurrent Layer

Recurrent networks are based on a more complex architecture designed to recursively handle an arbitrary number of context words. Recurrent NNLMs are described in (Mikolov et al., 2010; Mikolov et al., 2011b) and are experimentally shown to outperform both standard back-off LMs and feed-forward NNLMs in terms of perplexity on a small task. The key aspect of this architecture is that the input layer for predicting the ith word w_i in a text contains both a numeric representation $\mathbf{v}_{i-1}$ of the previous word and the hidden layer for the previous prediction.

The hidden layer thus acts as a representation of the context history that iteratively accumulates an unbounded number of previous words representations.

Our reimplementation of recurrent NNLMs slightly differs from the feed-forward architecture mainly by its input part.We use the same deep architecture to model the relation between the input word presentations and the input layer as in the recurrent model. However, we explicitly restrict the context to the $n-1$ previous words. Note that this architecture is just a convenient intermediate model that is used to efficiently train a recurrent model, as described in Section 3. In the recurrent model, the input layer is estimated as a recursive function of both the current input word and the past input layer.

$$\mathbf{i} = \text{sigm}(\mathbf{W}\mathbf{i}_{-1} + \mathbf{R}^T\mathbf{v_{-1}}) \tag{6}$$

As in the standard model, $\mathbf{R}^T\mathbf{v_{-k}}$ associates each context word $\mathbf{v_{-k}}$ to one feature vector (the corresponding row in $\mathbf{R}$). This vector plays the role of a bias at subsequent input layers. The input part is thus structured in a series of layers, the relation between the input layer and the first previous word being at level 1, the second previous word is at level 2 and so on. In (Mikolov et al., 2010; Mikolov et al., 2011b), recurrent models make use of the entire context, from the current word position all the way back to the beginning of the document. This greatly increases the complexity of training, as each document must be considered as a whole and processed position per position. By comparison, our reimplementation only considers a fixed context length, which can be increased at will, thus simulating a true recurrent architecture; this enables us to take advantage of several techniques during training that speed up learning (see Section 3). Furthermore, as discussed below, our preliminary results show that restricting the context to the current sentence is sufficient to attain optimal performance [2].

2.2 Structured Output Layer

A major difficulty with the neural network approach is the complexity of inference and training, which largely depends on the size of the output vocabulary ,i.e. of the number of words that have to be predicted. To overcome this problem, Le et al. (2011a) have proposed the structured Output Layer (SOUL) architecture. Following (Mnih and Hinton, 2008), the SOUL model combines the neural network approach with a class-based LM (Brown et al., 1992). Structuring the output layer and using word class information makes the estimation of distribution over large output vocabulary computationally feasible.

In the SOUL LM, the output vocabulary is structured in a clustering tree, where every word is associated to a unique path from the root node to a leaf node. Denoting w_i the ith word in a sentence, the sequence $c_{1:D}(w_i) = c_1, \dots, c_D$ encodes the path for word w_i in this tree, with D the tree depth, $c_d(w_i)$ the class or sub-class assigned to w_i, and $c_D(w_i)$ the leaf associated with w_i, comprising just the word itself. The probability of w_i given its history h can then be computed as:

$$P(w_i|h) = P(c_1(w_i)|h) \times \prod_{d=2}^{D} P(c_d(w_i)|h, c_{1:d-1}). \tag{7}$$

There is a softmax function at each level of the tree and each word ends up forming its own class (a leaf). The SOUL architecture is represented in the right part of Figure 1. The first *(class layer)* estimates the class probability $P(c_1(w_i)|h)$, while *sub-class layers* estimate the sub-class probabilities $P(c_d(w_i)|h, c_{1:d-1}), d = 2 \dots (D-1)$. Finally, the *word layer* estimates the word probabilities $P(c_D(w_i)|h, c_{1:D-1})$. As in (Schwenk, 2007), words in the short-list remain special, as each of them represents a (final) class on its own right.

3 Efficiency issues

Training a SOUL model can be achieved by maximizing the log-likelihood of the parameters on some training corpus. Following (Bengio et al., 2003), this optimization is performed by Stochastic Back-Propagation (SBP). Recurrent models are usually trained using a variant of SBP called the *Back-Propagation Through Time* (BPTT) (Rumelhart et al., 1986; Mikolov et al., 2011a).

Following (Schwenk, 2007), it is possible to greatly speed up the training of NNLMs using,

[2] The test sets used in MT experiments are made of various News extracts. Their content is thus not homogeneous and using words from previous sentences doesn't seem to be relevant.

for instance, n-gram level resampling and bunch mode training with parallelization (see below); these methods can drastically reduce the overall training time, from weeks to days. Adapting these methods to recurrent models are not straightforward. The same goes with the SOUL extension: its training scheme requires to first consider a restricted output vocabulary (the shortlist), that is then extended to include the complete prediction vocabulary (Le et al., 2011b). This technique is too time consuming, in practice, to be used when training recurrent models. By bounding the recurrence to a dozen or so previous words, we obtain a recurrent-like n-gram model that can benefit from a variety of speed-up techniques, as explained in the next sections.

Note that the bounded-memory approximation is only used for training: once training is complete, we derive a true recurrent network using the parameters trained on its approximation. This recurrent architecture is then used for inference.

3.1 Reducing the training data

Our usual approach for training large scale models is based on n-gram level *resampling* a subset of the training data at each epoch. This is not directly compatible with the recurrent model, which requires to iterate over the training data sentence-by-sentence in the same order as they occur in the document. However, by restricting the context to sentences, data resampling can be carried out at the sentence level. This means that the input layer is reinitialized at the beginning of each sentence so as to "forget", as it were, the memory of the previous sentences. A similar proposal is made in (Mikolov et al., 2011b), where the temporal dependencies are limited to the level of paragraph. Another useful trick, which is also adopted here, is to use different sampling rates for the various subparts of the data, thus boosting the use of in-domain versus out-of-domain data.

3.2 Bunch mode

Bunch mode training processes sentences by batches of several examples, thus enabling matrix operation that are performed very efficiently by the existing BLAS library. After resampling, the training data is divided into several sentence flows which are processed simultaneously. While the number of examples per batch can be as high as 128 without any visible loss of performance for n-gram NNLM, we found, after some preliminary experiments, that the value of 32 seems to yield a good tradeoff between the computing time and the performance for recurrent models. Using such batches, the training time can be speeded up by a factor of 8 at the price of a slight loss (less than 2%) in perplexity.

3.3 SOUL training scheme

The SOUL training scheme integrates several steps aimed at dealing with the fact that the output vocabulary is split in two sub-parts: very frequent words are in the so-called *short-list* and are treated differently from the less frequent ones. This setting can not be easily reproduced with recurrent models. By contrast, using the pseudo-recurrent n-gram NNLM, the SOUL training scheme can be adopted; the resulting parameter values are then plugged in into a truly recurrent architecture. In the light of the results reported below, we content ourselves with values of n in the range 8-10.

4 Experimental Results

We now turn to the experimental part, starting with a description of the experimental setup. We will then present an attempt to quantify the relative importance of history words, followed by a head to head comparison of the various NNLM architectures discussed in the previous sections.

4.1 Experimental setup

The tasks considered in our experiments are derived from the shared translation track of WMT 2011 (translation from English to French). We only provide here a short overview of the task; all the necessary details regarding this evaluation campaign are available on the official Web site[3] and our system is described in (Allauzen et al., 2011). Simply note that our parallel training data includes a large Web corpus, referred to as the *GigaWord parallel corpus*. After various preprocessing and filtering steps, the total amount of training data is approximately 12 million sentence pairs for the bilingual part, and about 2.5 billion of words for the monolingual part.

To built the target language models, the monolingual corpus was first split into several sub-parts

[3]http://www.statmt.org/wmt11

based on date and genre information. For each of these sub-corpora, a standard 4-gram LM was then estimated with interpolated Kneser-Ney smoothing (Chen and Goodman, 1996). All models were created without any pruning nor cutoff. The baseline back-off n-gram LM was finally built as a linear combination of several these models, where the interpolation coefficients are chosen so as to minimize the perplexity of a development set.

All NNLMs are trained following the prescriptions of Le et al. (2011b), and they all share the same inner structure: the dimension of the projection word space is 500; the size of two hidden layers are respectively 1000 and 500; the short-list contains 2000 words; and the non-linearity is introduced with the sigmoid function. For the recurrent model, the parameter that limits the back-propagation of errors through time is set to 9 (see (Mikolov et al., 2010) for details). This parameter can be considered to play a role that is similar to the history size in our pseudo-recurrent n-gram model: a value of 9 in the recurrent setting is equivalent to $n = 10$. All NNLMs are trained with the following resampling strategy: 75% of in-domain data (monolingual News data 2008-2011) and 25% of the other data. At each epoch, the parameters are updated using approximately 50 millions words for the last training step and about 140 millions words for the previous ones.

4.2 The usefulness of remote words

In this section, we analyze the influence of each context word with respect to their distance from the predicted word and to their POS tag. The quantitative analysis relies on the variant of the n-gram architecture based on (5) (see Section 2.1), which enables us to keep track of the most important context word for each prediction. Throughout this study, we will consider 10-gram NNLMs.

Figure 2 represents the selection rate with respect to the word position and displays the percentage of coordinates in the input layer that are selected for each position. As expected, close words are the most important, with the previous word accounting for more than 35% of the components. Remote words (at a distance between 7 and 9) have almost the same, weak, influence, with a selection rate close to 2.5%. This is consistent with the perplexity results of n-gram NNLMs as a function of n, reported in Table 2: the difference between all orders from 4-gram to 8-gram are significant, while the difference between 8-gram and 10-gram is negligible.

Tag	Meaning	Example
ABR	abreviation	etc FC FMI
ABK	other abreviation	ONG BCE CE
ADJ	adjective	officielles alimentaire mondial
ADV	adverb	contrairement assez alors
DET	article;	une les la
	possessive pronoun	ma ta
INT	interjection	oui adieu tic-tac
KON	conjunction	que et comme
NAM	proper name	Javier Mercure Pauline
NOM	noun	surprise inflation crise
NUM	numeral	deux cent premier
PRO	pronoun	cette il je
PRP	preposition;	de en dans
	preposition plus article	au du aux des
PUN	punctuation;	: , -
	punctuation citation	”
SENT	sentence tag	? . !
SYM	symbol	%
VER	verb	ont fasse parlent
<s>	start of sentence	

Table 1: *List of grouped tags from TreeTagger.*

POS tags were computed using the TreeTagger (Schmid, 1994); sub-types of a main tag are pooled to reduce the total number of categories. For example, all the tags for verbs are merged into the same VER class. Adding the token <s> (sentence start), our tagset contains 17 tags (see Table 1).

The average selection rates for each tag are shown in Figure 3: for each category, we display (in bars) the average number of components that correspond to a word in that category when this word is in previous position. Rare tags (INT, ABK , ABR and SENT) seem to provide a very useful information and have very high selection rates. Conversely, DET, PUN and PRP words occur relatively frequently and belong to the less selective group. The two most frequent tags (NOM and VER) have a medium selection rate (approximately 0.5).

4.3 Translation experiments

The integration of NNLMs for large SMT tasks is far from easy, given the computational cost of computing n-gram probabilities, a task that is performed repeatedly during the search of the best translation. Our solution was to resort to a two-pass approach: the first pass uses a conventional back-off n-gram model to produce a list of the k most likely translations; in the second pass, the NNLMs probability

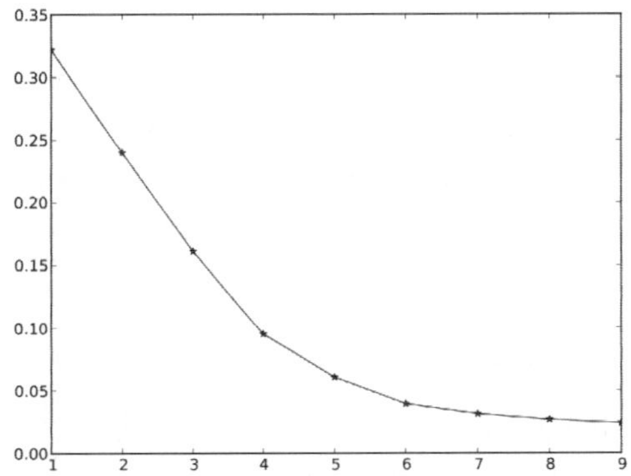

Figure 2: *Average selection rate per word position for the* max*-based NNLM, computed on newstest2009-2011. On x axis, the number k represents the kth previous word.*

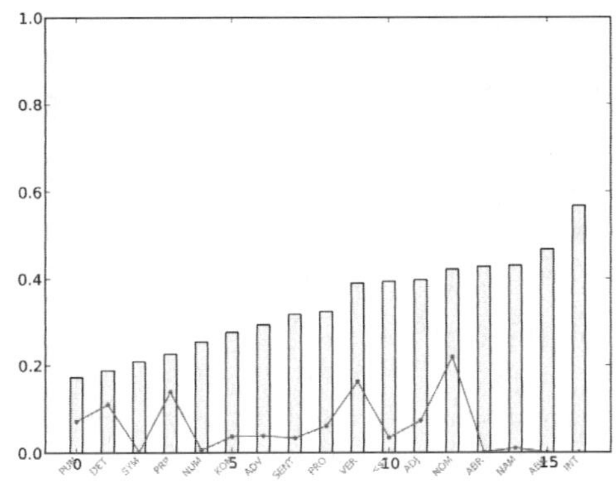

Figure 3: *Average selection rate of max function of the first previous word in terms of word POS-tag information, computed on newstest2009-2011. The green line represents the distribution of occurrences of each tag.*

of each hypothesis is computed and the k-best list is accordingly reordered. The NNLM weights are optimized as the other feature weights using Minimum Error Rate Training (MERT) (Och, 2003). For all our experiments, we used the value $k = 300$.

To clarify the impact of the language model order in translation performance, we considered three different ways to use NNLMs. In the first setting, the NNLM is used *alone* and all the scores provided by the MT system are ignored. In the second setting (*replace*), the NNLM score replaces the score of the standard back-off LM. Finally, the score of the NNLM can be added in the linear combination (*add*). In the last two settings, the weights used for

Model	Perplexity	BLEU		
		alone	*replace*	*add*
Baseline	90	29.4	31.3	-
4-gram	92	29.8	31.1	31.5
6-gram	82	30.2	31.6	**31.8**
8-gram	78	**30.6**	31.6	**31.8**
10-gram	**77**	30.5	**31.7**	**31.8**
recurrent	81	30.4	31.6	**31.8**

Table 2: *Results for the English to French task obtained with the baseline system and with various NNLMs. Perplexity is computed on newstest2009-2011 while BLEU is on the test set (newstest2010).*

n-best reranking are re-tuned with MERT.

Table 2 summarizes the BLEU scores obtained on the *newstest2010* test set. BLEU improvements are observed with feed-forward NNLMs using a value of $n = 8$ with respect to the baseline ($n = 4$). Further increase from 8 to 10 only provides a very small BLEU improvement. These results strengthen the assumption made in Section 3.3: *there seem to be very little information in remote words (above $n =$ 7-8)*. It is also interesting to see that the 4-gram NNLM achieves a comparable perplexity to the conventional 4-gram model, yet delivers a small BLEU increase in the *alone* condition.

Surprisingly[4], on this task, recurrent models seem to be comparable with 8-gram NNLMs. The reason may be the deep architecture of recurrent model that makes it hard to be trained in a large scale task. With the recurrent-like n-gram model described in Section 2.1.2, it is feasible to train a recurrent model on a large task. With 10% of perplexity reduction as compared to a backoff model, its yields comparable performances as reported in (Mikolov et al., 2011a). To the best of our knowledge, it is the first recurrent NNLM trained on a such large dataset (2.5 billion words) in a reasonable time (about 11 days).

5 Related work

There have been many attempts to increase the context beyond a couple of history words (see eg. (Rosenfeld, 2000)), for example: by modeling syn-

[4]Pers. com. with T. Mikolov: on the "small" WSJ data set, the recurrent model described in (Mikolov et al., 2011b) outperforms the 10-gram NNLM.

tactic information, that better reflects the "distance" between words (Chelba and Jelinek, 2000; Collins et al., 2005; Schwartz et al., 2011); with a unigram model of the whole history (Kuhn and Mori, 1990); by using trigger models (Lau et al., 1993); or by trying to model document topics (Seymore and Rosenfeld, 1997). One interesting proposal avoids the n-gram assumption by estimating the probability of a sentence (Rosenfeld et al., 2001). This approach relies on a maximum entropy model which incorporates arbitrary features. No significant improvements were however observed with this model, a fact that can be attributed to two main causes: first, the partition function can not be computed exactly as it involves a sum over all the possible sentences; second, it seems that data sparsity issues for this model are also adversely affecting the performance.

The recurrent network architecture for LMs was proposed in (Mikolov et al., 2010) and then extended in (Mikolov et al., 2011b). The authors propose a hierarchical architecture similar to the SOUL model, based however on a simple unigram clustering. For large scale tasks ($\approx 400M$ training words), advanced training strategies were investigated in (Mikolov et al., 2011a). Instead of resampling, the data was divided into paragraphs, filtered and then sorted: the most in-domain data was thus placed at the end of each epoch. On the other hand, the hidden layer size was decreased by simulating a maximum entropy model using a hash function on n-grams. This part represents direct connections between input and output layers. By sharing the prediction task, the work of the hidden layer is made simpler, and can thus be handled with a smaller number of hidden units. This approach reintroduces into the model discrete features which are somehow one main weakness of conventional backoff LMs as compared to NNLMs. In fact, this strategy can be viewed as an effort to directly combine the two approaches (backoff-model and neural network), instead of using a traditional way, through interpolation. Training simultaneously two different models is computationally very demanding for large vocabularies, even with help of hashing technique; in comparison, our approach keeps the model architecture simple, making it possible to use the efficient techniques developed for n-gram NNLMs.

The use the $\max$, rather than a sum, on the hidden layer of neural network is not new. Within the context of language modeling, it was first proposed in (Collobert et al., 2011) with the goal to model a variable number of input features. Our motivation for using this variant was different, and was mostly aimed at analyzing the influence of context words based on the selection rates of this function.

6 Conclusion

In this paper, we have investigated several types of NNLMs, along with conventional LMs, in order to assess the influence of long range dependencies within sentences in the language modeling task: from recurrent models that can recursively handle an arbitrary number of context words to n-gram NNLMs with n varying between 4 and 10. Our contribution is two-fold.

First, experimental results showed that the influence of word further than 9 can be neglected for the statistical machine translation task [5]. Therefore, the n-gram assumption with $n \approx 10$ appears to be well-founded to handle most sentence internal dependencies. Another interesting conclusion of this study is that the main issue of the conventional n-gram model is not its conditional independence assumptions, but the use of too small values for n.

Second, by restricting the context of recurrent networks, the model can benefit of the advanced training schemes and its training time can be divided by a factor 8 without loss on the performances. To the best of our knowledge, it is the first time that a recurrent NNLM is trained on a such large dataset in a reasonable time. Finally, we compared these models within a large scale MT task, with monolingual data that contains 2.5 billion words. Experimental results showed that using long range dependencies ($n = 10$) with a SOUL language model significantly outperforms conventional LMs. In this setting, the use of a recurrent architecture does not yield any improvements, both in terms of perplexity and BLEU.

Acknowledgments

This work was achieved as part of the Quaero Programme, funded by OSEO, the French State agency for innovation.

[5]The same trend is observed in speech recognition.

References

Alexandre Allauzen, Gilles Adda, Hélène Bonneau-Maynard, Josep M. Crego, Hai-Son Le, Aurélien Max, Adrien Lardilleux, Thomas Lavergne, Artem Sokolov, Guillaume Wisniewski, and François Yvon. 2011. LIMSI @ WMT11. In *Proceedings of the Sixth Workshop on Statistical Machine Translation*, pages 309–315, Edinburgh, Scotland.

Y Bengio, R Ducharme, P Vincent, and C Jauvin. 2003. A neural probabilistic language model. *Journal of Machine Learning Research*, 3(6):1137–1155.

Thorsten Brants, Ashok C. Popat, Peng Xu, Franz J. Och, and Jeffrey Dean. 2007. Large language models in machine translation. In *Proceedings of the 2007 Joint Conference on Empirical Methods in Natural Language Processing and Computational Natural Language Learning (EMNLP-CoNLL)*, pages 858–867.

Peter F. Brown, Peter V. deSouza, Robert L. Mercer, Vincent J. Della Pietra, and Jenifer C. Lai. 1992. Class-based n-gram models of natural language. *Comput. Linguist.*, 18(4):467–479.

Ciprian Chelba and Frederick Jelinek. 2000. Structured language modeling. *Computer Speech and Language*, 14(4):283–332.

Stanley F. Chen and Joshua Goodman. 1996. An empirical study of smoothing techniques for language modeling. In *Proc. ACL'96*, pages 310–318, San Francisco.

Michael Collins, Brian Roark, and Murat Saraclar. 2005. Discriminative syntactic language modeling for speech recognition. In *Proceedings of the 43rd Annual Meeting of the Association for Computational Linguistics (ACL'05)*, pages 507–514, Ann Arbor, Michigan, June. Association for Computational Linguistics.

Ronan Collobert and Jason Weston. 2008. A unified architecture for natural language processing: deep neural networks with multitask learning. In *Proc. of ICML'08*, pages 160–167, New York, NY, USA. ACM.

Ronan Collobert, Jason Weston, Léon Bottou, Michael Karlen, Koray Kavukcuoglu, and Pavel Kuksa. 2011. Natural language processing (almost) from scratch. *Journal of Machine Learning Research*, 12:2493–2537.

Ahmad Emami, Imed Zitouni, and Lidia Mangu. 2008. Rich morphology based n-gram language models for arabic. In *INTERSPEECH*, pages 829–832.

R. Kuhn and R. De Mori. 1990. A cache-based natural language model for speech recognition. *IEEE Transactions on Pattern Analysis and Machine Intelligence*, 12(6):570–583, june.

Hong-Kwang Kuo, Lidia Mangu, Ahmad Emami, and Imed Zitouni. 2010. Morphological and syntactic features for arabic speech recognition. In *Proc. ICASSP 2010*.

Raymond Lau, Ronald Rosenfeld, and Salim Roukos. 1993. Adaptive language modeling using the maximum entropy principle. In *Proc HLT'93*, pages 108–113, Princeton, New Jersey.

Hai-Son Le, Ilya Oparin, Alexandre Allauzen, Jean-Luc Gauvain, and François Yvon. 2011a. Structured output layer neural network language model. In *Proceedings of ICASSP'11*, pages 5524–5527.

Hai-Son Le, Ilya Oparin, Abdel. Messaoudi, Alexandre Allauzen, Jean-Luc Gauvain, and François Yvon. 2011b. Large vocabulary SOUL neural network language models. In *Proceedings of InterSpeech 2011*.

Xunying Liu, Mark J. F. Gales, and Philip C. Woodland. 2011. Improving lvcsr system combination using neural network language model cross adaptation. In *INTERSPEECH*, pages 2857–2860.

Tomáš Mikolov, Martin Karafiát, Lukáš Burget, Jan Černocký, and Sanjeev Khudanpur. 2010. Recurrent neural network based language model. In *Proceedings of the 11th Annual Conference of the International Speech Communication Association (INTERSPEECH 2010)*, volume 2010, pages 1045–1048. International Speech Communication Association.

Tomáš Mikolov, Anoop Deoras, Daniel Povey, Lukáš Burget, and Jan Černocký. 2011a. Strategies for training large scale neural network language models. In *Proceedings of ASRU 2011*, pages 196–201. IEEE Signal Processing Society.

Tomáš Mikolov, Stefan Kombrink, Lukas Burget, Jan Cernocký, and Sanjeev Khudanpur. 2011b. Extensions of recurrent neural network language model. In *Proc. of ICASSP'11*, pages 5528–5531.

Andriy Mnih and Geoffrey E Hinton. 2008. A scalable hierarchical distributed language model. In D. Koller, D. Schuurmans, Y. Bengio, and L. Bottou, editors, *Advances in Neural Information Processing Systems 21*, volume 21, pages 1081–1088.

Franz Josef Och. 2003. Minimum error rate training in statistical machine translation. In *Proceedings of the 41st Annual Meeting on Association for Computational Linguistics - Volume 1*, ACL '03, pages 160–167, Stroudsburg, PA, USA. Association for Computational Linguistics.

Ronald Rosenfeld, Stanley F. Chen, and Xiaojin Zhu. 2001. Whole-sentence exponential language models: A vehicle for linguistic-statistical integration. *Computers, Speech and Language*, 15:2001.

R. Rosenfeld. 2000. Two decades of statistical language modeling: Where do we go from here ? *Proceedings of the IEEE*, 88(8).

D. E. Rumelhart, G. E. Hinton, and R. J. Williams. 1986. Parallel distributed processing: explorations in the microstructure of cognition, vol. 1. chapter Learning internal representations by error propagation, pages 318–362. MIT Press, Cambridge, MA, USA.

Helmut Schmid. 1994. Probabilistic part-of-speech tagging using decision trees. In *Proceedings of International Conference on New Methods in Language Processing*.

Lane Schwartz, Chris Callison-Burch, William Schuler, and Stephen Wu. 2011. Incremental syntactic language models for phrase-based translation. In *Proceedings of the 49th Annual Meeting of the Association for Computational Linguistics: Human Language Technologies*, pages 620–631, Portland, Oregon, USA, June. Association for Computational Linguistics.

Holger Schwenk and Jean-Luc Gauvain. 2002. Connectionist language modeling for large vocabulary continuous speech recognition. In *Proc. ICASSP*, pages 765–768, Orlando, FL.

H. Schwenk and P. Koehn. 2008. Large and diverse language models for statistical machine translation. In *International Joint Conference on Natural Language Processing*, pages 661–666, Janv 2008.

Holger Schwenk. 2007. Continuous space language models. *Comput. Speech Lang.*, 21(3):492–518.

Kristie Seymore and Ronald Rosenfeld. 1997. Using story topics for language model adaptation. In *Proc. of Eurospeech '97*, pages 1987–1990, Rhodes, Greece.

Yeh W. Teh. 2006. A hierarchical Bayesian language model based on Pitman-Yor processes. In *Proc. of ACL'06*, pages 985–992, Sidney, Australia.

Large, Pruned or Continuous Space Language Models on a GPU for Statistical Machine Translation

Holger Schwenk, Anthony Rousseau and Mohammed Attik
LIUM, University of Le Mans
72085 Le Mans cedex 9, FRANCE
Holger.Schwenk@lium.univ-lemans.fr

Abstract

Language models play an important role in large vocabulary speech recognition and statistical machine translation systems. The dominant approach since several decades are back-off language models. Some years ago, there was a clear tendency to build huge language models trained on hundreds of billions of words. Lately, this tendency has changed and recent works concentrate on data selection. Continuous space methods are a very competitive approach, but they have a high computational complexity and are not yet in widespread use. This paper presents an experimental comparison of all these approaches on a large statistical machine translation task. We also describe an open-source implementation to train and use continuous space language models (CSLM) for such large tasks. We describe an efficient implementation of the CSLM using graphical processing units from Nvidia. By these means, we are able to train an CSLM on more than 500 million words in 20 hours. This CSLM provides an improvement of up to 1.8 BLEU points with respect to the best back-off language model that we were able to build.

1 Introduction

Language models are used to estimate the probability of a sequence of words. They are an important module in many areas of natural language processing, in particular large vocabulary speech recognition (LVCSR) and statistical machine translation (SMT). The goal of LVCSR is to convert a speech signal x into a sequence of words w. This is usually approached with the following fundamental equation:

$$\begin{aligned} w^* &= \arg\max_w P(w|x) \\ &= \arg\max_w P(x|w)P(w) \end{aligned} \qquad (1)$$

In SMT, we are faced with a sequence of words e in the source language and we are looking for its best translation f into the target language. Again, we apply Bayes rule to introduce a language model:

$$\begin{aligned} f^* &= \arg\max_f P(f|e) \\ &= \arg\max_f P(e|f)P(f) \end{aligned} \qquad (2)$$

Although we use a language model to evaluate the probability of the produced sequence of words, w and f respectively, we argue that the task of the language model is not exactly the same for both applications. In LVCSR, the LM must choose among a large number of possible segmentations of the phoneme sequence into words, given the pronunciation lexicon. It is also the only component that helps to select among homonyms, i.e. words that are pronounced in the same way, but that are written differently and which have usually different meanings (e.g. *ate/eight* or *build/billed*). In SMT, on the other hand, the LM has the responsibility to chose the best translation of a source word given the context. More importantly, the LM is a key component which has to sort out good and bad word reorderings. This is known to be a very difficult issue when translating from or into languages like Chinese, Japanese or German. In LVCSR, the word order is given by the time-synchronous processing of the speech signal. Finally, the LM helps to deal with gender, number, etc accordance of morphologically rich languages, when used in an LVCSR as well as an SMT system. Overall, one can say that the semantic level seems to be more important for language modeling in SMT than LVCSR. In both applications, so called back-off n-gram language models are the de facto standard since several decades. They were first introduced in the eighties, followed by intensive research on smoothing methods. An extensive comparison can be found in (Chen and Goodman, 1999). Modified-Kneser Ney smoothing seems to be the best performing method and it is this approach that is almost exclusively used today.

Some years ago, there was a clear tendency in SMT to use huge LMs trained on hundreds on billions (10^11) of words (Brants et al., 2007). The authors report continuous improvement of the translation quality with increasing size of the LM training data, but these models require a large cluster to train and to perform inference using distributed storage. Therefore, several approaches were proposed to limit the storage size of large LMs, for instance (Federico and Cettolo, 2007; Talbot and Osborne, 2007; Heafield, 2011).

1.1 Continuous space language models

The main drawback of back-off n-gram language models is the fact that the probabilities are estimated in a discrete space. This prevents any kind of interpolation in order to estimate the LM probability of an n-gram which was not observed in the training data. In order to attack this problem, it was proposed to project the words into a continuous space and to perform the estimation task in this space. The projection as well as the estimation can be jointly performed by a multi-layer neural network (Bengio and Ducharme, 2001; Bengio et al., 2003). The basic architecture of this approach is shown in figure 1.

A standard fully-connected multi-layer perceptron is used. The inputs to the neural network are the indices of the $n-1$ previous words in the vocabulary $h_j=w_{j-n+1}, \ldots, w_{j-2}, w_{j-1}$ and the outputs are the posterior probabilities of *all* words of the vocabulary:

$$P(w_j = i|h_j) \qquad \forall i \in [1, N] \tag{3}$$

where N is the size of the vocabulary. The input uses the so-called 1-of-n coding, i.e., the ith word of

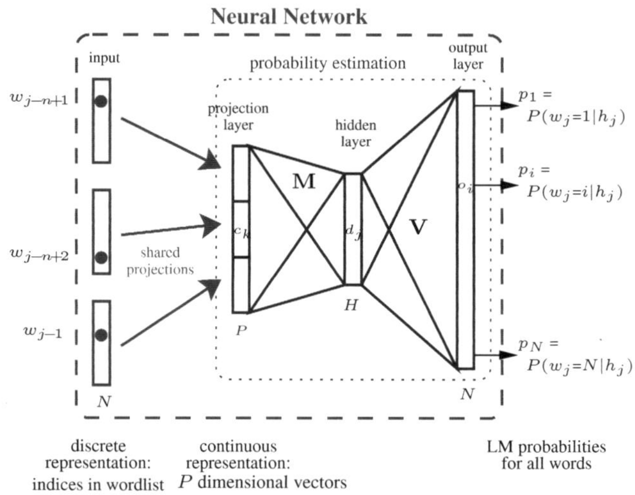

Figure 1: Architecture of the continuous space LM. h_j denotes the context $w_{j-n+1}, \ldots, w_{j-1}$. P is the size of one projection and H,N is the size of the hidden and output layer respectively. When short-lists are used the size of the output layer is much smaller then the size of the vocabulary.

the vocabulary is coded by setting the ith element of the vector to 1 and all the other elements to 0. The ith line of the $N \times P$ dimensional projection matrix corresponds to the continuous representation of the ith word. Let us denote c_l these projections, d_j the hidden layer activities, o_i the outputs, p_i their softmax normalization, and m_{jl}, b_j, v_{ij} and k_i the hidden and output layer weights and the corresponding biases. Using these notations, the neural network performs the following operations:

$$d_j = \tanh\left(\sum_l m_{jl}\, c_l + b_j\right) \tag{4}$$

$$o_i = \sum_j v_{ij}\, d_j + k_i \tag{5}$$

$$p_i = e^{o_i} \Big/ \sum_{r=1}^{N} e^{o_r} \tag{6}$$

The value of the output neuron p_i is used as the probability $P(w_j = i|h_j)$. Training is performed with the standard back-propagation algorithm minimizing the following error function:

$$E = \sum_{i=1}^{N} t_i \log p_i + \beta \left(\sum_{jl} m_{jl}^2 + \sum_{ij} v_{ij}^2\right) \tag{7}$$

where t_i denotes the desired output, i.e., the probability should be 1.0 for the next word in the training sentence and 0.0 for all the other ones. The first part of this equation is the cross-entropy between the output and the target probability distributions, and the second part is a regularization term that aims to prevent the neural network from overfitting the training data (weight decay). The parameter β has to be determined experimentally.

The CSLM has a much higher complexity than a back-off LM, in particular because of the high dimension of the output layer. Therefore, it was proposed to limit the size of the output layer to the most frequent words, the other ones being predicted by a standard back-off LM (Schwenk, 2004). All the words are still considered at the input layer.

It is important to note that the CSLM is still an n-gram approach, but the notion of backing-off to shorter contexts does not exist any more. The model can provide probability estimates for any possible n-gram. It also has the advantage that the complexity only slightly increases for longer context windows, while it is generally considered to be unfeasible to train back-off LMs on billions of words for orders larger than 5.

The CSLM was very successfully applied to large vocabulary speech recognition. It is usually used to rescore lattices and improvements of the word error rate of about one point were consistently observed for many languages and domains, for instance (Schwenk and Gauvain, 2002; Schwenk, 2007; Park et al., 2010; Liu et al., 2011; Lamel et al., 2011). More recently, the CSLM was also successfully applied to statistical machine translation (Schwenk et al., 2006; Schwenk and Estève, 2008; Schwenk, 2010; Le et al., 2010)

During the last years, several extensions were proposed in the literature, for instance:

- Mikolov and his colleagues are working on the use of recurrent neural networks instead of multi-layer feed-forward architecture (Mikolov et al., 2010; Mikolov et al., 2011).
- A simplified calculation of the short-list probability mass and the addition of an adaptation layer (Park et al., 2010; Liu et al., 2011)
- the so-called SOUL architecture which allows to cover all the words at the output layer instead of using a short-list (Le et al., 2011a; Le et al., 2011b), based on work by (Morin and Bengio, 2005; Mnih and Hinton, 2008).
- alternative sampling in large corpora (Xu et al., 2011)

Despite significant and consistent gains in LVCSR and SMT, CSLMs are not yet in widespread use. Possible reasons for this could be the large computational complexity which requires flexible and carefully tuned software so that the models can be build and used in an efficient manner.

In this paper we provide a detailed comparison of the current most promising language modeling techniques for SMT: huge back-off LMs that integrate all available data, LMs trained on data selected with respect to its relevance to the task by a recently proposed method (Moore and Lewis, 2010), and a new very efficient implementation of the CSLM which integrates data selection.

2 Continuous space LM toolkit

Free software to train and use CSLM was proposed in (Schwenk, 2010). The first version of this toolkit provided no support for short lists or other means to train CSLMs with large output vocabularies. Therefore, it was not possible to use it for LVCSR and large SMT tasks. We extended our tool with full support for short lists during training and inference. Short lists are implemented as proposed in (Park et al., 2010), i.e. we add one extra output neuron for all words that are not in the short list. This probability mass is learned by the neural network from the training data. However, we do not use this probability mass to renormalize the output distribution, we simply assume that it is sufficiently close to the probability mass reserved by the back-off LM for words that are not in the short list. In summary, during inference words in the short-list are predicted by the neural network and all the other ones by a standard back-off LM. No renormalization is performed. We have performed some comparative experiments with renormalization during inference and we could not observe significant differences. The toolkit supports LMs in the SRILM format, an interface to the popular KENLM is planed.

2.1 Parallel processing

The computational power of general purpose processors like those build by Intel or AMD has constantly increased during the last decades and optimized libraries are available to take advantage of the multi-core capabilities of modern CPUs. Our CSLM toolkit fully supports parallel processing based on Intel's MKL library.[1] Figure 2 shows the time used to train a large neural network on 1M examples. We trained a 7-gram CSLM with a projection layer of size 320, two hidden layers of size 1024 and 512 respectively, and an output layer of dimension 16384 (short-list). We compared two hardware architectures:

- a top-end PC with one Intel Core i7 3930K processor (3.2 GHz, 6 cores).
- a typical server with two Intel Xeon X5675 processors (2× 3.06 GHz, 6 cores each).

We did not expect a linear increase of the speed with the number of threads run in parallel, but nevertheless, there is a clear benefit of using multiple cores: processing is about 6 times faster when running on 12 cores instead of a single one. The Core i7 3930K processor is actually slightly faster than the Xeon X5675, but we are limited to 6 cores since it can not interact with a second processor.

2.2 Running on a GPU

In parallel to the development efforts for fast general purpose CPUs, dedicated hardware has been developed in order to satisfy the computational needs of realistic 3D graphics in high resolutions, so called graphical processing units (GPU). Recently, it was realized that this computational power can be in fact used for scientific computing, e.g. in chemistry, molecular physics, earth quake simulations, weather forecasts, etc. A key factor was the availability of libraries and toolkits to simplify the programming of GPU cards, for instance the CUDA toolkit of Nvidia.[2] The machine learning community has started to use GPU computing and several toolkits are available to train generic networks. We have also added support for Nvidia GPU cards to the

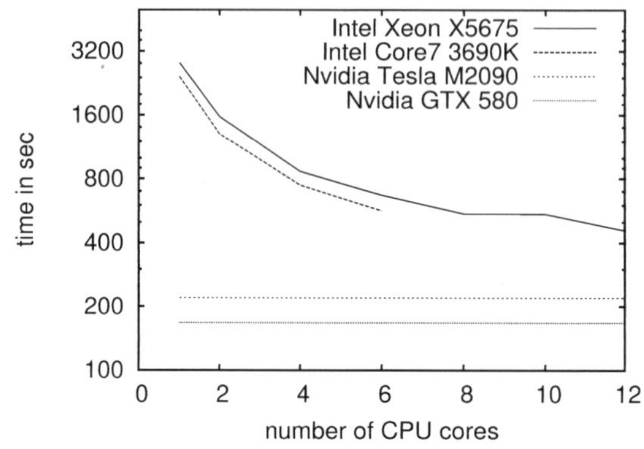

Figure 2: Time to train on 1M examples on various hardware architectures (the speed is shown in log scale).

CSLM toolkit. Timing experiments were performed with two types of GPU cards:

- a Nvidia GTX 580 GPU card with 3 GB of memory. It has 512 cores running at 1.54 GHz.
- a Nvidia Tesla M2090 card with 6 GB of memory. It has 512 cores running at 1.3 GHz.

As can be seen from figure 2, for these network sizes the GTX 580 is about 3 times faster than two Intel X5675 processors (12 cores). This speed-up is smaller than the ones observed in other studies to run machine learning tasks on a GPU, probably because of the large number of parameters which require many accesses to the GPU memory. For synthetic benchmarks, all the code and data often fits into the fast shared memory of the GPU card. We are continuing our work to improve the speed of our toolkit on GPU cards. The Tesla M2090 is a little bit slower than the GTX 580 due to the lower core frequency. However, it has a much better support for double precision floating point calculations which could be quite useful when training large neural networks.

3 Experimental Results

In this work, we present comparative results for various LMs when integrated into a large-scale SMT system to translate from Arabic into English. We use the popular Moses toolkit to build the SMT system (Koehn et al., 2007). As in our previous works, the CSLM is used to rescore 1000-best lists. The sentence probability calculated by the CSLM is added

[1] http://software.intel.com/en-us/articles/intel-mkl
[2] http://developer.nvidia.com/cuda-downloads

	AFP			APW			NYT			XIN			LTW	WPB	CNA
	old	avrg	recent	old	avrg	recent	old	avrg	recent	old	avrg	recent	all	all	all
Using all the data:															
Words	151M	547M	371M	385M	547M	444M	786M	543M	364M	105M	147M	144M	313M	20M	39M
Perplex	167.7	141.0	138.6	192.7	170.3	163.4	234.1	203.5	197.1	162.9	126.4	121.8	170.3	269.3	266.5
After data selection:															
Words	36M 23%	77M 26%	96M 26%	62M 16%	77M 14%	89M 20%	110M 14%	54M 10%	44M 12%	23M 22%	35M 24%	38M 26%	69M 22%	6M 30%	7M 18%
Perplex	160.9	135.0	131.6	185.3	153.2	151.1	201.2	173.6	169.5	159.6	123.4	117.7	153.1	263.9	253.2

Table 1: Perplexities on the development data (news wire genre) of the individual sub-corpora in the LDC Gigaword corpus, before and after data selection by the method of (Moore and Lewis, 2010).

as 15th feature function and the coefficients of all the feature functions are optimized by MERT. The CSLM toolkit includes scripts to perform this task.

3.1 Baseline systems

The Arabic/English SMT system was trained on parallel and monolingual data similar to those available in the well known NIST OpenMT evaluations. About 151M words of bitexts are available from LDC out of which we selected 41M words to build the translation model. The English side of all the bitexts was used to train the target language model.

In addition, we used the LDC Gigaword corpus version 5 (LDC2011T07). It contains about 4.9 billion words coming from various news sources (AFP and XIN news agencies, New York Times, etc) for the period 1994 until 2010. All corpus sizes are given after tokenization.

For development and tuning, we used the OpenMT 2009 data set which contains 1313 sentences. The corresponding data from 2008 was used as internal test set. We report separate results for the news wire part (586 sentence, 24k words) and the web part (727 sentences, 24k words) since we want to compare the performance of the various LMs for formal and more informal language. Four reference translations were available. Case and punctuation were preserved for scoring.

It is well known that it is better to build LMs on the individual sources and to interpolate them, instead of building one LM on all the concatenated data. The interpolation coefficients are tuned by optimizing the perplexity on the development corpus using an EM procedure. We split the huge Gigaword corpora AFP, APW, NYT and XIN into three parts according to the time period (old, average and recent). This gives in total 15 sub-corpora. The sizes and the perplexities are given in Table 1. The interpolated 4-gram LM of these 15 corpora has a perplexity of 87 on the news part.

If we add the English side of all the bitexts, the perplexity can be lowered to 71.1. All the observed n-grams were preserved, e.g. the cut-off for n-gram counts was set to 1 for all orders. This gives us an huge LM with 1.4 billion 4-grams, 548M 3-grams and 83M bigrams which requires more 26 GBytes to be stored on disk. This LM is loaded into memory by the Moses decoder. This takes more than 10 minutes and requires about 70 GB of memory.

Moses supports memory mapped LMs, like IRSTLM or KENLM, but this was not explored in this study. We call this LM "*big LM*". We believe that it could be considered as a very strong baseline for a back-off LM. We did not attempt to build higher order back-off LM given the size requirements. For comparison, we also build a small LM which was trained on the English part of the bitexts and the recent XIN corpus only. It has a perplexity of 78.9 and occupies 2 GB on disk (see table 2).

3.2 Data selection

We have reimplemented the method of Moore and Lewis (2010) to select the most appropriate LM data based on the difference between the sentence-wise entropy of an in-domain and out-of domain LM.

In our experiments, we have observed exactly the same behavior than reported by the authors: the perplexity decreases when less, but more appropriate

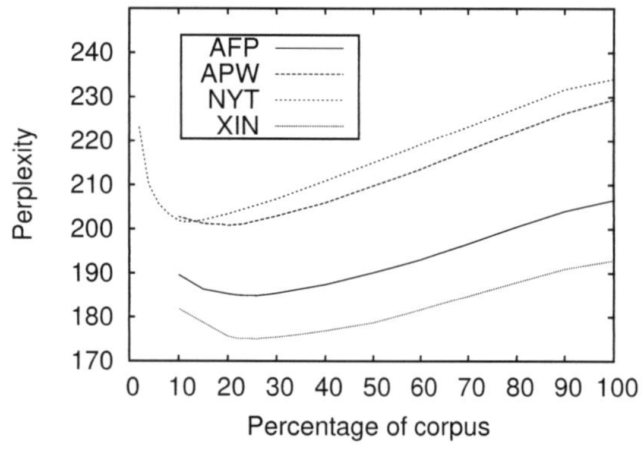

Figure 3: Decrease in perplexity when selecting data with the method proposed in (Moore and Lewis, 2010).

data is used, reaching a minimum using about 20% of the data only. The improvement in the perplexity can reach 20% relative. Figure3 shows the perplexity for some corpora in function of the size of the selected data. Detailed statistics for all corpora are given in Table 1 for the news genre.

Unfortunately, these improvements in perplexity almost vanish when we interpolate the individual language models: the perplexity is 86.6 instead of 87.0 when all the data from the Gigaword corpus is used. This LM achieves the same BLEU score on the development data, and there is a small improvement of 0.24 BLEU on the test set (Table 2). Nevertheless, the last LM has the advantage of being much smaller: 7.2 instead of 25 GBytes. We have also performed the data selection on the concatenated texts of 4.9 billion words. In this case, we do observe an decrease of the perplexity with respect to a model trained on all the concatenated data, but overall, the perplexity is higher than with an interpolated LM (as expected).

LM	Px Dev	Size	BLEU Dev	BLEU Test
Small	78.9	2.0 GB	56.89	49.66
Big	71.1	26 GB	58.66	50.75
Giga	87.0	25.0 GB	57.08	50.08
GigaSel	86.6	7.2 GB	57.03	50.32

Table 2: Comparison of several 4-gram back-off language models. See text for explanation of the models.

3.3 Continuous space language models

The CSLM was trained on all the available data using the resampling algorithm described in (Schwenk, 2007). At each epoch we randomly resampled about 15M examples. We build only one CSLM resampling simultaneously in all the corpora. The short list was set to 16k – this covers about 92% of the n-gram requests. Since it is very easy to use large context windows with an CSLM, we trained right away 7-grams. We provide a comparison of different context lengths later in this section. The networks were trained for 20 epochs. This can be done in about 64 hours on a server with two Intel X5675 processors and in 20 hours on a GPU card.

This CSLM achieves a perplexity of 62.9, to be compared to 71.1 for the big back-off LM. This is a relative improvement of more than 11%, but actually we can do better. If we train the CSLM on the *small corpus* only, i.e. the English side of the bitexts and the recent part of the XIN corpus, we achieve a perplexity of 61.9 (see table 3). This clearly indicates that it is better to focus the CSLM on relevant data.

Random resampling is a possibility to train a neural network on very large corpora, but it does not guarantee that all the examples are used. Even if we resampled different examples at each epoch, we would process at most 300M different examples (20 epochs times 15M examples). There is no reason to believe that we randomly select examples which are appropriate to the task (note, however, that the resampling coefficients are different for the individual

LM	Corpus size	Sent. select.	Perplex on Dev
Back-off 4-gram LM:			
Small	196M	no	78.9
Big	5057M	no	71.1
CSLM 7-gram:			
big	5057M	no	62.9
Small	196M	no	61.9
Small	92M	yes	60.9
6x Giga	425M	yes.	57.9
10x Giga	553M	yes.	**56.9**

Table 3: Perplexity on the development data (news genre) for back-off and continuous space language models.

Genre	Small LM 4-gram back-off	Huge LM	CSLM 7-gram
News	49.66	50.75	**52.28**
Web	/	35.17	**36.53**

Table 4: BLEU scores on the test set for the translation from Arabic into English for various language models.

Order:	4-gram	5-gram	6-gram	7-gram
Px Dev:	63.9	59.5	57.6	56.9
BLEU Dev:	59.76	60.11	60.29	60.26
BLEU Test:	51.91	51.85	52.23	52.28

Table 5: Perplexity on the development data (news genre) and BLEU scores of the continuous space language models in function of the context size.

corpora similar to the coefficients of an interpolated back-off LM). Therefore, we propose to use the data selection method of Moore and Lewis (2010) to concentrate the training of the CSLM on the most informative examples. Instead of sampling randomly n-grams in all the corpora, we do this in the selected data by the method of (Moore and Lewis, 2010). By these means, it is more likely that we train the CSLM on relevant data. Note that this has no impact on the training speed since the amount of resampled data is not changed.

The results for this method are summarized in Table 3. In a first experiment, we used the selected part of the recent XIN corpus only. This reduces the perplexity to 60.9. In addition, if we use the six or ten most important Gigaword corpora, we achieve a perplexity of 57.9 and 56.9 respectively. This is 10% better than resampling blindly in all the data (62.9 $\rightarrow$ 56.9). Overall, the 7-gram CSLM improves the perplexity by 20% relative with respect to the huge 4-gram back-off LM (71.1 $\rightarrow$ 56.9).

Finally, we used our best CSLM to rescore the n-best lists of the Arabic/English SMT system. The baseline BLEU score on the test set, news genre, is 49.66 with the small LM. This increases to 50.75 with the big LM. It was actually necessary to open the beam of the Moses decoder in order to observe such an improvement. The large beam had no effect when the small LM was used. This is a very strong baseline to improve upon. Nevertheless, this result is further improved by the CSLM to 52.28, i.e. a significant gain of 1.8 BLEU. We observe similar behavior for the WEB genre.

All our networks have two hidden layers since we have observed that this slightly improves performance with respect to the standard architecture with only one hidden layer. This is a first step towards so-called deep neural networks (Bengio, 2007), but we have not yet explored this systematically.

In an 1000-best list for 586 sentences, we have a total of 14M requests for 7-grams out of which more than 13.5M were processed by the CSLM, e.g. the short list hit rate is almost 95%. This resulted in only 2670 forward passes through the network. At each pass, we collected in average 5350 probabilities at the output layer. The processing takes only a couple of minutes on a server with two Xeon X5675 CPUs.

One can of course argue that it is not correct to compare 4-gram and 7-gram language models. However, building 5-gram or higher order back-off LMs on 5 billion words is computationally very expensive, in particular with respect to memory usage. For comparison, we also trained lower order CSLM models. It can be clearly seen from Table 5 that the CSLM can take advantage of longer contexts, but it already achieves a significant improvement in the BLEU score at the same LM order (BLEU on the test data: 50.75 $\rightarrow$ 51.91).

The CSLM is very space efficient: a saved network occupies about 600M on disk in function of the network architecture, in particular in function of the size of the continuous projection. Loading takes only a couple of seconds. During training, 1 GByte of main memory is sufficient. The memory requirement during n-best rescoring essentially depends on the back-off LM that is eventually charged to deal with out-off short-list words. Figure 4 shows some example translations.

4 Conclusion

This paper presented a comparison of several popular techniques to build language models for statistical machine translation systems: huge back-off models trained on billions of words, data selection of most relevant examples and a highly efficient implementation of continuous space methods.

Huge LMs perform well, but their storage may require important computational resources – in our

كما تفقد الوزير المركز الفرعي المتكامل لمكافحة التلوث البحري بالزيت الذي يشتمل علي أحدث معدات مواجهة التلوث البحري وتفقد المعمل الكيميائي بالميناء المتخصص في مراقبة الجودة للزيت الخام والمزود بأحدث الأجهزة التكنولوجية الحديثة.

Back-off LM:The minister inspected the sub-committee integrated combat marine pollution with oil, which includes the latest equipment lose face marine pollution and chemical plant in the port specializing in monitoring the quality of the crude oil supplier and with the most modern technological devices.

CSLM: The minister inspected the integrated sub-committee to combat marine pollution with oil, which includes the latest equipment deal with marine pollution and inspect the chemical plant in the port specializing in monitoring the quality of the crude oil supplier, with the most modern technological devices.

Google: The minister also inspected the sub-center for integrated control of marine pollution with oil, which includes the latest equipment on the face of marine pollution and chemical plant loses port specialist in quality control of crude oil and supplied

بيونغيانغ تعد باحترام التزاماتها لانهاء البرنامج النووي

Back-off LM:Pyongyang is to respect its commitments to end nuclear program.

CSLM: Pyongyang promised to respect its commitments to end the nuclear program.

Google: Pyongyang is to respect its obligations to end nuclear program.

قام مسلحو طالبان بعمليات الاختطاف فى البلاد بشكل متكرر خلال العامين الماضيين .

Back-off LM: The Taliban militants in kidnappings in the country over the past two years.

CSLM: Taliban militants have carried out kidnappings in the country repeatedly during the past two years.

Google:The Taliban kidnappings in the country frequently over the past two years.

Figure 4: Example translations when using the huge back-off and the continuous space LM. For comparison we also provide the output of Google Translate.

case, 26 GB on disk and 70 GB of main memory for a model trained on 5 billions words. The data selection method proposed in (Moore and Lewis, 2010) is very effective at the corpus level, but the observed gains almost vanish after interpolation. However, the storage requirement can be divided by four.

The main contributions of this paper are several improvements of the continuous space language model. We have shown that data selection is very useful to improve the resampling of training data in large corpora. Our best model achieves a perplexity reduction of 20% relative with respect to the best back-off LM we were able to build. This gives an improvement of up to 1.8 BLEU points in a very competitive Arabic/English statistical machine translation system.

We have also presented a very efficient implementation of the CSLM. The tool can take advantage of modern multi-core or multi-processor computers. We also support graphical extension cards like the Nvidia 3D graphic cards. By these means, we are able to train a CSLM on 500M words in about 20 hours. This tool is freely available.[3] By these means we hope to make large-scale continuous space language modeling available to a larger community.

[3]http://www-lium.univ-lemans.fr/~cslm

Acknowledgments

This work has been partially funded by the French Government under the project COSMAT (ANR-09-CORD-004) and the European Commission under the project FP7 EuromatrixPlus.

References

Yoshua Bengio and Rejean Ducharme. 2001. A neural probabilistic language model. In *NIPS*, volume 13, pages 932–938.

Yoshua Bengio, Rejean Ducharme, Pascal Vincent, and Christian Jauvin. 2003. A neural probabilistic language model. *JMLR*, 3(2):1137–1155.

Yoshua Bengio. 2007. learning deep architectures for AI. Technical report, University of Montréal.

Thorsten Brants, Ashok C. Popat, Peng Xu, Franz J. Och, and Jeffrey Dean. 2007. Large language models in machine translation. In *EMNLP*, pages 858–867.

Stanley F. Chen and Joshua T. Goodman. 1999. An empirical study of smoothing techniques for language modeling. *Computer Speech & Language*, 13(4):359–394.

Marcello Federico and Maura Cettolo. 2007. Efficient handling of n-gram language models for statistical machine translation. In *Second Workshop on SMT*, pages 88–95.

Kenneth Heafield. 2011. KenLM: Faster and smaller language model queries. In *Sixth Workshop on SMT*, pages 187–197.

Philipp Koehn, Hieu Hoang, Alexandra Birch, Chris Callison-Burch, Marcello Federico, Nicola Bertoldi, Brooke Cowan, Wade Shen, Christine Moran, Richard Zens, Chris Dyer, Ondrej Bojar, Alexandra Constantin, and Evan Herbst. 2007. Moses: Open source toolkit for statistical machine translation. In *ACL, demonstration session*.

L. Lamel, J.-L. Gauvain, V.-B. Le, I. Oparin, , and S. Meng. 2011. Improved models for mandarin speech-to-text transcription. In *ICASSP*, pages 4660–4663.

H.S. Le, A. Allauzen, G. Wisniewski, and F. Yvon. 2010. Training continuous space language models: Some practical issues. In *EMNLP*, pages 778–788.

H.S. Le, I. Oparin, A. Allauzen, J-L. Gauvain, and F. Yvon. 2011a. Structured output layer neural network language model. In *ICASSP*, pages 5524–5527.

H.S. Le, I. Oparin, A. Messaoudi, A. Allauzen, J-L. Gauvain, and F. Yvon. 2011b. Large vocabulary SOUL neural network language models. In *Interspeech*.

X. Liu, M. J. F. Gales, and P. C. Woodland. 2011. Improving LVCSR system combination using neural network language model cross adaptation. In *Interspeech*, pages 2857–2860.

Tomáš Mikolov, Martin Karafiát, Lukáš Burget, Jan Černocký, and Sanjeev Khudanpur. 2010. Recurrent neural network based language model. In *Interspeech*, pages 1045–1048.

T. Mikolov, S. Kombrink, L. Burget, J.H. Cernocky, and S. Khudanpur. 2011. Extensions of recurrent neural network language model. In *ICASSP*, pages 5528–5531.

Andriy Mnih and Geoffrey Hinton. 2008. A scalable hierarchical distributed language model. In *NIPS*.

Robert C. Moore and William Lewis. 2010. Intelligent selection of language model training data. In *ACL*, pages 220–224.

Frederic Morin and Yoshua Bengio. 2005. Hierarchical probabilistic neural network language model. In *Proceedings of the Tenth International Workshop on Artificial Intelligence and Statistics*.

Junho Park, Xunying Liu, Mark J. F. Gales, and Phil C. Woodland. 2010. Improved neural network based language modelling and adaptation. In *Interspeech*, pages 1041–1044.

Holger Schwenk and Yannick Estève. 2008. Data selection and smoothing in an open-source system for the 2008 NIST machine translation evaluation. In *Interspeech*, pages 2727–2730.

Holger Schwenk and Jean-Luc Gauvain. 2002. Connectionist language modeling for large vocabulary continuous speech recognition. In *ICASSP*, pages I: 765–768.

Holger Schwenk, Daniel Déchelotte, and Jean-Luc Gauvain. 2006. Continuous space language models for statistical machine translation. In *Proceedings of the COLING/ACL 2006 Main Conference Poster Sessions*, pages 723–730.

Holger Schwenk. 2004. Efficient training of large neural networks for language modeling. In *IJCNN*, pages 3059–3062.

Holger Schwenk. 2007. Continuous space language models. *Computer Speech and Language*, 21:492–518.

Holger Schwenk. 2010. Continuous space language models for statistical machine translation. *The Prague Bulletin of Mathematical Linguistics*, (93):137–146.

David Talbot and Miles Osborne. 2007. Smoothed bloom filter language models: Tera-scale lms on the cheap. In *EMNLP*, pages 468–476.

Puyang Xu, Asela Gunawardana, and Sanjeev Khudanpur. 2011. Efficient subsampling for training complex language models. In *EMNLP*, pages 1128–1136.

Deep Neural Network Language Models

Ebru Arısoy, Tara N. Sainath, Brian Kingsbury, Bhuvana Ramabhadran
IBM T.J. Watson Research Center
Yorktown Heights, NY, 10598, USA
{earisoy, tsainath, bedk, bhuvana}@us.ibm.com

Abstract

In recent years, neural network language models (NNLMs) have shown success in both peplexity and word error rate (WER) compared to conventional n-gram language models. Most NNLMs are trained with one hidden layer. Deep neural networks (DNNs) with more hidden layers have been shown to capture higher-level discriminative information about input features, and thus produce better networks. Motivated by the success of DNNs in acoustic modeling, we explore deep neural network language models (DNN LMs) in this paper. Results on a Wall Street Journal (WSJ) task demonstrate that DNN LMs offer improvements over a single hidden layer NNLM. Furthermore, our preliminary results are competitive with a model M language model, considered to be one of the current state-of-the-art techniques for language modeling.

1 Introduction

Statistical language models are used in many natural language technologies, including automatic speech recognition (ASR), machine translation, handwriting recognition, and spelling correction, as a crucial component for improving system performance. A statistical language model represents a probability distribution over all possible word strings in a language. In state-of-the-art ASR systems, n-grams are the conventional language modeling approach due to their simplicity and good modeling performance. One of the problems in n-gram language modeling is data sparseness. Even with large training corpora, extremely small or zero probabilities can be assigned to many valid word sequences. Therefore, smoothing techniques (Chen and Goodman, 1999) are applied to n-grams to reallocate probability mass from observed n-grams to unobserved n-grams, producing better estimates for unseen data.

Even with smoothing, the discrete nature of n-gram language models make generalization a challenge. What is lacking is a notion of word similarity, because words are treated as discrete entities. In contrast, the neural network language model (NNLM) (Bengio et al., 2003; Schwenk, 2007) embeds words in a continuous space in which probability estimation is performed using single hidden layer neural networks (feed-forward or recurrent). The expectation is that, with proper training of the word embedding, words that are semantically or gramatically related will be mapped to similar locations in the continuous space. Because the probability estimates are smooth functions of the continuous word representations, a small change in the features results in a small change in the probability estimation. Therefore, the NNLM can achieve better generalization for unseen n-grams. Feed-forward NNLMs (Bengio et al., 2003; Schwenk and Gauvain, 2005; Schwenk, 2007) and recurrent NNLMs (Mikolov et al., 2010; Mikolov et al., 2011b) have been shown to yield both perplexity and word error rate (WER) improvements compared to conventional n-gram language models. An alternate method of embedding words in a continuous space is through tied mixture language models (Sarikaya et al., 2009), where n-grams frequencies are modeled similar to acoustic features.

To date, NNLMs have been trained with one hidden layer. A *deep* neural network (DNN) with multiple hidden layers can learn more higher-level, abstract representations of the input. For example, when using neural networks to process a raw pixel representation of an image, lower layers might detect different edges, middle layers detect more complex but local shapes, and higher layers identify abstract categories associated with sub-objects and objects which are parts of the image (Bengio, 2007). Recently, with the improvement of computational resources (i.e. GPUs, mutli-core CPUs) and better training strategies (Hinton et al., 2006), DNNs have demonstrated improved performance compared to shallower networks across a variety of pattern recognition tasks in machine learning (Bengio, 2007; Dahl et al., 2010).

In the acoustic modeling community, DNNs have proven to be competitive with the well-established Gaussian mixture model (GMM) acoustic model. (Mohamed et al., 2009; Seide et al., 2011; Sainath et al., 2012). The depth of the network (the number of layers of nonlinearities that are composed to make the model) and the modeling a large number of context-dependent states (Seide et al., 2011) are crucial ingredients in making neural networks competitive with GMMs.

The success of DNNs in acoustic modeling leads us to explore DNNs for language modeling. In this paper we follow the feed-forward NNLM architecture given in (Bengio et al., 2003) and make the neural network deeper by adding additional hidden layers. We call such models deep neural network language models (DNN LMs). Our preliminary experiments suggest that deeper architectures have the potential to improve over single hidden layer NNLMs.

This paper is organized as follows: The next section explains the architecture of the feed-forward NNLM. Section 3 explains the details of the baseline acoustic and language models and the set-up used for training DNN LMs. Our preliminary results are given in Section 4. Section 5 summarizes the related work to our paper. Finally, Section 6 concludes the paper.

2 Neural Network Language Models

This section describes a general framework for feed-forward NNLMs. We will follow the notations given in (Schwenk, 2007).

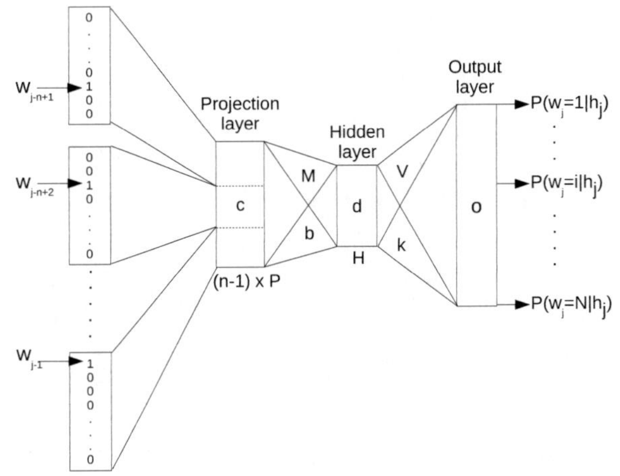

Figure 1: Neural network language model architecture.

Figure 1 shows the architecture of a neural network language model. Each word in the vocabulary is represented by a N dimensional sparse vector where only the index of that word is 1 and the rest of the entries are 0. The input to the network is the concatenated discrete feature representations of n-1 previous words (history), in other words the indices of the history words. Each word is mapped to its continuous space representation using linear projections. Basically discrete to continuous space mapping is a look-up table with N x P entries where N is the vocabulary size and P is the feature dimension. i'th row of the table corresponds to the continuous space feature representation of i'th word in the vocabulary. The continuous feature vectors of the history words are concatenated and the projection layer is performed. The hidden layer has H hidden units and it is followed by hyperbolic tangent nonlinearity. The output layer has N targets followed by the softmax function. The output layer posterior probabilities, $P(w_j = i|h_j)$, are the language model probabilities of each word in the output vocabulary for a specific history, h_j.

Let's c represents the linear activations in the projection layer, M represents the weight matrix between the projection and hidden layers and V represents the weight matrix between the hidden and output layers, the operations in the neural network are as follows:

$$d_j = \tanh\left(\sum_{l=1}^{(n-1)\times P} M_{jl}c_l + b_j\right) \forall j = 1, \cdots, H$$

$$o_i = \sum_{j=1}^{H} V_{ij}d_j + k_i \; \forall i = 1, \cdots, N$$

$$p_i = \frac{\exp(o_i)}{\sum_{r=1}^{N}\exp(o_r)} = P(w_j = i|h_j)$$

where b_j and k_i are the hidden and output layer biases respectively.

The computational complexity of this model is dominated by HxN multiplications at the output layer. Therefore, a shortlist containing only the most frequent words in the vocabulary is used as the output targets to reduce output layer complexity. Since NNLM distribute the probability mass to only the target words, a background language model is used for smoothing. Smoothing is performed as described in (Schwenk, 2007). Standard back-propagation algorithm is used to train the model.

Note that NNLM architecture can also be considered as a neural network with two hidden layers. The first one is a hidden layer with linear activations and the second one is a hidden layer with nonlinear activations. Through out the paper we refer the first layer the projection layer and the second layer the hidden layer. So the neural network architecture with a single hidden layer corresponds to the NNLM, and is also referred to as a single hidden layer NNLM to distinguish it from DNN LMs.

Deep neural network architecture has several layers of nonlinearities. In DNN LM, we use the same architecture given in Figure 1 and make the network deeper by adding hidden layers followed by hyperbolic tangent nonlinearities.

3 Experimental Set-up

3.1 Baseline ASR system

While investigating DNN LMs, we worked on the WSJ task used also in (Chen 2008) for model M language model. This set-up is suitable for our initial experiments since having a moderate size vocabulary minimizes the effect of using a shortlist at the output layer. It also allows us to compare our preliminary results with the state-of-the-art performing model M language model.

The language model training data consists of 900K sentences (23.5M words) from 1993 WSJ text with verbalized punctuation from the CSR-III Text corpus, and the vocabulary is the union of the training vocabulary and 20K-word closed test vocabulary from the first WSJ CSR corpus (Paul and Baker, 1992). For speech recognition experiments, a 3-gram modified Kneser-Ney smoothed language model is built from 900K sentences. This model is pruned to contain a total of 350K n-grams using entropy-based pruning (Stolcke, 1998) .

Acoustic models are trained on 50 hours of Broadcast news data using IBM Attila toolkit (Soltau et al., 2010). We trained a cross-word quinphone system containing 2,176 context-dependent states and a total of 50,336 Gaussians.

From the verbalized punctuation data from the training and test portions of the WSJ CSR corpus, we randomly select 2,439 unique utterances (46,888 words) as our evaluation set. From the remaining verbalized punctuation data, we select 977 utterances (18,279 words) as our development set.

We generate lattices by decoding the development and test set utterances with the baseline acoustic models and the pruned 3-gram language model. These lattices are rescored with an unpruned 4-gram language model trained on the same data. After rescoring, the baseline WER is obtained as 20.7% on the held-out set and 22.3% on the test set.

3.2 DNN language model set-up

DNN language models are trained on the baseline language model training text (900K sentences). We chose the 10K most frequent words in the vocabulary as the output vocabulary. 10K words yields 96% coverage of the test set. The event probabilities for words outside the output vocabulary were smoothed as described in (Schwenk, 2007). We used the unpruned 4-gram language model as the background language model for smoothing. The input vocabulary contains the 20K words used in baseline n-gram model. All DNN language models are 4-gram models. We experimented with different projection layer sizes and numbers of hidden units, using the same number of units for each hidden layer. We trained DNN LMs up to 4 hidden layers. Unless otherwise noted, the DNN LMs are not pre-trained, i.e. the weights are initialized randomly, as previous work has shown deeper networks have more impact on improved performance compared to pre-training (Seide et al., 2011).

The cross-entropy loss function is used during training, also referred to as fine-tuning or backpropagation. For each epoch, all training data is randomized. A set of 128 training instances, referred to as a mini-batch, is selected randomly without replacement and weight updates are made on this mini-batch. After one pass through the training data, loss is measured on a held-out set of 66.4K words and the learning rate is annealed (i.e. reduced) by a factor of 2 if the held-out loss has not improved sufficiently over the previous iteration. Training stops after we have annealed the weights 5 times. This training recipe is similar to the recipe used in acoustic modeling experiments (Sainath et al., 2012).

To evaluate our language models in speech recognition, we use lattice rescoring. The lattices generated by the baseline acoustic and language models are rescored using 4-gram DNN language models. The acoustic weight for each model is chosen to optimize word error rate on the development set.

4 Experimental Results

Our initial experiments are on a single hidden layer NNLM with 100 hidden units and 30 dimensional features. We chose this configuration for our initial experiments because this models trains in one day of training on an 8-core CPU machine. However, the performance of this model on both the held-out and test sets was worse than the baseline. We therefore increased the number of hidden units to 500, while keeping the 30-dimensional features. Training a single hidden layer NNLM with this configuration required approximately 3 days on an 8-core CPU machine. Adding additional hidden layers does not have as much an impact in the training time as increased units in the output layer. This is because the computational complexity of a DNN LM is dominated by the computation in the output layer. However, increasing the number of hidden units does impact the training time. We also experimented with different number of dimensions for the features, namely 30, 60 and 120. Note that these may not be the optimal model configurations for our

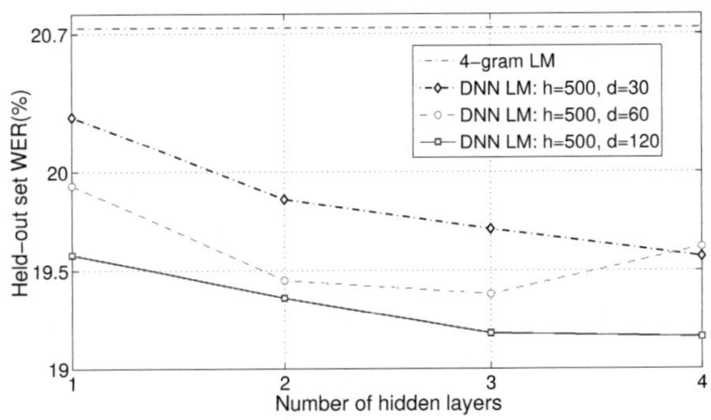

Figure 2: Held-out set WERs after rescoring ASR lattices with 4-gram baseline language model and 4-gram DNN language models containing up to 4 hidden layers.

set-up. Exploring several model configurations can be very expensive for DNN LMs, we chose these parameters arbitrarily based on our previous experience with NNLMs.

Figure 2 shows held-out WER as a function of the number of hidden layers for 4-gram DNN LMs with different feature dimensions. The same number of hidden units is used for each layer. WERs are obtained after rescoring ASR lattices with the DNN language models only. We did not interpolate DNN LMs with the 4-gram baseline language model while exploring the effect of additional layers on DNN LMs. The performance of the 4-gram baseline language model after rescoring (20.7%) is shown with a dashed line. h denotes the number of hidden units for each layer and d denotes the feature dimension at the projection layer. DNN LMs containing only a single hidden layer corresponds to the NNLM. Note that increasing the dimension of the features improves NNLM performance. The model with 30 dimensional features has 20.3% WER, while increasing the feature dimension to 120 reduces the WER to 19.6%. Increasing the feature dimension also shifts the WER curves down for each model. More importantly, Figure 2 shows that using deeper networks helps to improve the performance. The 4-layer DNN LM with 500 hidden units and 30 dimensional features (DNN LM: $h = 500$ and $d = 30$) reduces the WER from 20.3% to 19.6%. For a DNN LM with 500 hidden units and 60 dimensional features (DNN LM: $h = 500$ and $d = 60$), the 3-layer model yields the best performance and reduces the WER from 19.9% to 19.4%. For DNN LM with 500 hidden units and 120 dimensional features (DNN LM: $h = 500$ and $d = 120$), the WER curve plateaus after the 3-layer model. For this model the WER reduces from 19.6% to 19.2%.

We evaluated models that performed best on the held-out set on the test set, measuring both perplexity and WER. The results are given in Table 1. Note that perplexity and WER for all the models were calculated using the model by itself, without interpolating with a baseline n-gram language model. DNN LMs have lower perplexities than their single hidden layer counterparts. The DNN language models for each configuration yield 0.2-0.4% absolute improvements in WER over NNLMs. Our best result on the test set is obtained with a 3-layer DNN LM with 500 hidden units and 120 dimensional features. This model yields 0.4% absolute improvement in WER over the NNLM, and a total of 1.5% absolute improvement in WER over the baseline 4-gram language model.

Table 1: Test set perplexity and WER.

Models	Perplexity	WER(%)
4-gram LM	114.4	22.3
DNN LM: h=500, d=30		
with 1 layer (NNLM)	115.8	22.0
with 4 layers	108.0	21.6
DNN LM: h=500, d=60		
with 1 layer (NNLM)	109.3	21.5
with 3 layers	105.0	21.3
DNN LM: h=500, d=120		
with 1 layer (NNLM)	104.0	21.2
with 3 layers	102.8	20.8
Model M (Chen, 2008)	99.1	20.8
RNN LM (h=200)	99.8	-
RNN LM (h=500)	83.5	-

Table 1 shows that DNN LMs yield gains on top of NNLM. However, we need to compare deep networks with shallow networks (i.e. NNLM) with the same number of parameters in order to conclude that DNN LM is better than NNLM. Therefore, we trained different NNLM architectures with varying projection and hidden layer dimensions. All of these models have roughly the same number of parameters (8M) as our best DNN LM model, 3-layer DNN LM with 500 hidden units and 120 dimensional features. The comparison of these models is given in Table 2. The best WER is obtained with DNN LM, showing that deep architectures help in language modeling.

Table 2: Test set perplexity and WER. The models have 8M parameters.

Models	Perplexity	WER(%)
NNLM: h=740, d=30	114.5	21.9
NNLM: h=680, d=60	108.3	21.3
NNLM: h=500, d=140	103.8	21.2
DNN LM: h=500, d=120 with 3 layers	102.8	20.8

We also compared our DNN LMs with a model M LM and a recurrent neural network LM (RNNLM) trained on the same data, considered to be current state-of-the-art techniques for language modeling. Model M is a class-based exponential language model which has been shown to yield significant improvements compared to conventional n-gram language models (Chen, 2008; Chen et al., 2009). Because we used the same set-up as (Chen, 2008), model M perplexity and WER are reported directly in Table 1. Both the 3-layer DNN language model and model M achieve the same WER on the test set; however, the perplexity of model M is lower.

The RNNLM is the most similar model to DNN LMs because the RNNLM can be considered to have a deeper architecture thanks to its recurrent connections. However, the RNNLM proposed in (Mikolov et al., 2010) has a different architecture at the input and output layers than our DNN LMs. First, RNNLM does not have a projection layer. DNN LM has $N \times P$ parameters in the look-up table and a weight matrix containing $(n-1) \times P \times H$ parameters between the projection and the first hidden layers. RNNLM has a weight matrix containing $(N+H) \times H$ parameters between the input and the hidden layers. Second, RNNLM uses the full vocabulary (20K words) at the output layer, whereas, DNN LM uses a shortlist containing 10K words. Because of the number of output targets in RNNLM, it results in more parameters even with the same number of hidden units with DNN LM. Note that the additional hidden layers in DNN LM will introduce extra parameters. However, these parameters will have a little effect compared to $10,000 \times H$ additional parameters introduced in RNNLM due to the use of the full vocabulary at the output layer.

We only compared DNN and RNN language models in terms of perplexity since we can not directly use RNNLM in our lattice rescoring framework. We trained two models using the RNNLM toolkit[1], one with 200 hidden units and one with 500 hidden units. In order to speed up training, we used 150 classes at the output layer as described in (Mikolov et al., 2011b). These models have 8M and 21M parameters respectively. RNNLM with 200 hidden units has the same number of parameters with our best DNN LM model, 3-layer DNN LM with 500 hidden units and 120 dimensional features. The results are given in Table 1. This model results in a lower perplexity than DNN LMs. RNNLM with 500 hidden units results in the best perplexity in Table 1 but it has much more parameters than DNN LMs. Note that, RNNLM uses the full history and DNN LM uses only the 3-word context as the history. Therefore, increasing the n-gram context can help to improve the performance for DNN LMs.

We also tested the performance of NNLM and DNN LM with 500 hidden units and 120-dimensional features after linearly interpolating with the 4-gram baseline language model. The interpolation weights were chosen to minimize the perplexity on the held-out set. The results are given Table 3. After linear interpolation with the 4-gram baseline language model, both the perplexity and WER improve for NNLM and DNN LM. However, the gain with 3-layer DNN LM on top of NNLM diminishes.

Table 3: Test set perplexity and WER with the interpolated models.

Models	Perplexity	WER(%)
4-gram LM	114.4	22.3
4-gram + DNN LM: (h=500, d=120)		
with 1 layer (NNLM)	93.1	20.6
with 3 layers	92.6	20.5

One problem with deep neural networks, especially those with more than 2 or 3 hidden layers, is that training can easily get stuck in local minima, resulting in poor solutions. Therefore, it may be important to apply pre-training (Hinton et al., 2006) instead of randomly initializing the weights. In this paper we investigate discriminative pre-training for DNN LMs. Past work in acoustic modeling has shown that performing discriminative pre-training followed by fine-tuning allows for fewer iterations of fine-tuning and better model performance than generative pre-training followed by fine-tuning (Seide et al., 2011).

In discriminative pre-training, a NNLM (one projection layer, one hidden layer and one output layer) is trained using the cross-entropy criterion. After one pass through the training data, the output layer weights are discarded and replaced by another randomly initialized hidden layer and output layer. The initially trained projection and hidden layers are held constant, and discriminative pre-training is performed on the new hidden and output layers. This discriminative training is performed greedy and layer-wise like generative pre-training.

After pre-training the weights for each layer, we explored two different training (fine-tuning) scenarios. In the first one, we initialized all the layers, including the output layer, with the pre-trained weights. In the second one, we initialized all the layers, except the output layer, with the pre-trained weights. The output layer weights are initialized randomly. After initializing the weights for each layer, we applied our standard training recipe.

Figure 3 and Figure 4 show the held-out WER as a function of the number of hidden layers for the case of no pre-training and the two discriminative pre-training scenarios described above using models with 60- and 120-dimensional features. In the figures, pre-training 1 refers to the first scenario and pre-training 2 refers to the second scenario. As seen in the figure, pre-training did not give consistent gains for models with different number of hidden layers. We need to investigate discriminative pre-training and other pre-training strategies further for DNN LMs.

5 Related Work

NNLM was first introduced in (Bengio et al., 2003) to deal with the challenges of n-gram language models by learning the distributed representations of

[1] http://www.fit.vutbr.cz/~imikolov/rnnlm/

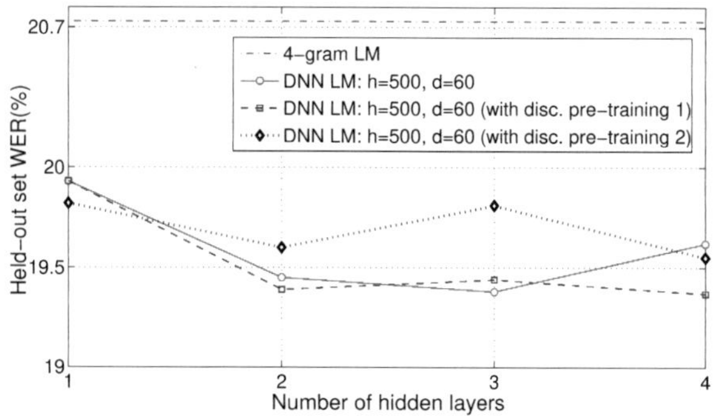

Figure 3: Effect of discriminative pre-training for DNN LM: h=500, d=60.

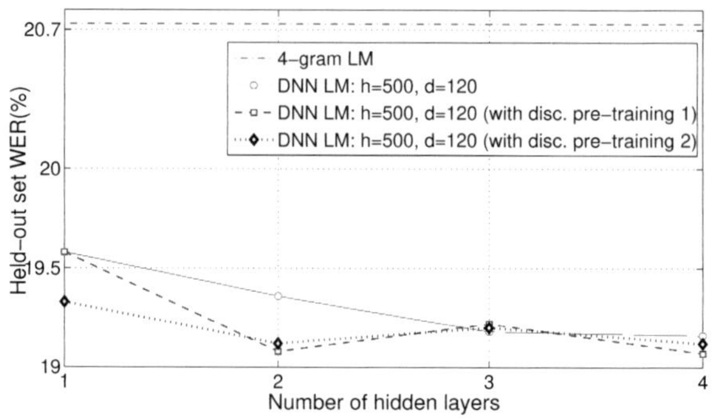

Figure 4: Effect of discriminative pre-training for DNN LM: h=500, d=120.

words together with the probability function of word sequences. This NNLM approach is extended to large vocabulary speech recognition in (Schwenk and Gauvain, 2005; Schwenk, 2007) with some speed-up techniques for training and rescoring. Since the input structure of NNLM allows for using larger contexts with a little complexity, NNLM was also investigated in syntactic-based language modeling to efficiently use long distance syntactic information (Emami, 2006; Kuo et al., 2009). Significant perplexity and WER improvements over smoothed n-gram language models were reported with these efforts.

Performance improvement of NNLMs comes at the cost of model complexity. Determining the output layer of NNLMs poses a challenge mainly attributed to the computational complexity. Using a shortlist containing the most frequent several thousands of words at the output layer was proposed (Schwenk, 2007), however, the number of hidden units is still a restriction. Hierarchical decomposition of conditional probabilities has been proposed to speed-up NNLM training. This decomposition is performed by partitioning output vocabulary words into classes or by structuring the output layer to multiple levels (Morin and Bengio, 2005; Mnih and Hinton, 2008; Son Le et al., 2011). These approaches provided significant speed-ups in training and make the training of NNLM with full vocabularies computationally feasible.

In the NNLM architecture proposed in (Bengio et al., 2003), a feed-forward neural network with a single hidden layer was used to calculate the language model probabilities. Recently, a recurrent neural network architecture was proposed for language modelling (Mikolov et al., 2010). In contrast to the fixed content in feed-forward NNLM, recurrent connections allow the model to use arbitrarily long histories. Using classes at the output layer was also investigated for RNNLM to speed-up the training (Mikolov et al., 2011b). It has been shown that significant gains can be obtained on top of a very good state-of-the-art system after scaling up RNNLMs in terms of data and model sizes (Mikolov et al., 2011a).

There has been increasing interest in using neural networks also for acoustic modeling. Hidden Markov Models (HMMs), with state output distributions given by Gaussian Mixture Models (GMMs) have been the most popular methodology for acoustic modeling in speech recognition for the past 30 years. Recently, deep neural networks (DNNs) (Hinton et al., 2006) have been explored as an alternative to GMMs to model state output distributions. DNNs were first explored on a small vocabulary phonetic recognition task, showing a 5% relative improvement over a state-of-the-art GMM/HMM baseline system (Dahl et al., 2010). Recently, DNNs have been extended to large vocabulary tasks, showing a 10% relative improvement over a GMM/HMM system on an English Broadcast News task (Sainath et al., 2012), and a 25% relative improvement on a conversational telephony task (Seide et al., 2011).

As summarized, recent NNLM research has focused on making NNLMs more efficient. Inspired by the success of acoustic modeling with DNNs, we applied deep neural network architectures to language modeling. To our knowledge, DNNs have not been investigated before for language modeling. RNNLMs are the closest to our work since recurrent connections can be considered as a deep architecture where weights are shared across hidden layers.

6 Conclusion and Future Work

In this paper we investigated training language models with deep neural networks. We followed the feed-forward neural network architecture and made the network deeper with the addition of several layers of nonlinearities. Our preliminary experiments on WSJ data showed that deeper networks can also be useful for language modeling. We also compared shallow networks with deep networks with the same number of parameters. The best WER was obtained with DNN LM, showing that deep architectures help in language modeling. One important observation in our experiments is that perplexity and WER improvements are more pronounced with the increased projection layer dimension in NNLM than the increased number of hidden layers in DNN LM. Therefore, it is important to investigate deep architectures with larger projection layer dimensions to see if deep architectures are still useful. We also investigated discriminative pre-training for DNN LMs, however, we do not see consistent gains. Different pre-training strategies, including generative methods, need to be investigated for language modeling.

Since language modeling with DNNs has not been investigated before, there is no recipe for building DNN LMs. Future work will focus on elaborating training strategies for DNN LMs, including investigating deep architectures with different number of hidden units and pre-training strategies specific for language modeling. Our results are preliminary but they are encouraging for using DNNs in language modeling.

Since RNNLM is the most similar in architecture to our DNN LMs, it is important to compare these two models also in terms of WER. For a fair comparison, the models should have similar n-gram contexts, suggesting a longer context for DNN LMs. The increased depth of the neural network typically allows learning more patterns from the input data. Therefore, deeper networks can allow for better modeling of longer contexts.

The goal of this study was to analyze the behavior of DNN LMs. After finding the right training recipe for DNN LMs in WSJ task, we are going to compare DNN LMs with other language modeling approaches in a state-of-the-art ASR system where the language models are trained with larger amounts of data. Training DNN LMs with larger amounts of data can be computationally expensive, however, classing the output layer as described in (Mikolov et al., 2011b; Son Le et al., 2011) may help to speed up training.

References

Yoshua Bengio, Rejean Ducharme, Pascal Vincent, and Christian Jauvin. 2003. A neural probabilistic language model. *Journal of Machine Learning Research*, 3:1137–1155.

Yoshua Bengio. 2007. Learning Deep Architectures for AI. Technical report, Universit e de Montreal.

S. F. Chen and J. Goodman. 1999. An empirical study of smoothing techniques for language modeling. *Computer Speech and Language*, 13(4).

Stanley F. Chen, Lidia Mangu, Bhuvana Ramabhadran, Ruhi Sarikaya, and Abhinav Sethy. 2009. Scaling shrinkage-based language models. In *Proc. ASRU 2009*, pages 299–304, Merano, Italy, December.

Stanley F. Chen. 2008. Performance prediction for exponential language models. Technical Report RC 24671, IBM Research Division.

George E. Dahl, Marc'Aurelio Ranzato, Abdel rahman Mohamed, and Geoffrey E. Hinton. 2010. Phone Recognition with the Mean-Covariance Restricted Boltzmann Machine. In *Proc. NIPS*.

Ahmad Emami. 2006. *A neural syntactic language model*. Ph.D. thesis, Johns Hopkins University, Baltimore, MD, USA.

Geoffrey E. Hinton, Simon Osindero, and Yee-Whye Teh. 2006. A Fast Learning Algorithm for Deep Belief Nets. *Neural Computation*, 18:1527–1554.

H-K. J. Kuo, L. Mangu, A. Emami, I. Zitouni, and Y-S. Lee. 2009. Syntactic features for Arabic speech recognition. In *Proc. ASRU 2009*, pages 327 – 332, Merano, Italy.

Tomas Mikolov, Martin Karafiat, Lukas Burget, Jan Cernocky, and Sanjeev Khudanpur. 2010. Recurrent neural network based language model. In *Proc. INTERSPEECH 2010*, pages 1045–1048.

Tomas Mikolov, Anoop Deoras, Daniel Povey, Lukas Burget, and Jan Cernocky. 2011a. Strategies for training large scale neural network language models. In *Proc. ASRU 2011*, pages 196–201.

Tomas Mikolov, Stefan Kombrink, Lukas Burget, Jan Cernocky, and Sanjeev Khudanpur. 2011b. Extensions of recurrent neural network language model. In *Proc. ICASSP 2011*, pages 5528–5531.

Andriy Mnih and Geoffrey Hinton. 2008. A scalable hierarchical distributed language model. In *Proc. NIPS*.

Abdel-rahman Mohamed, George E. Dahl, and Geoffrey Hinton. 2009. Deep belief networks for phone recognition. In *Proc. NIPS Workshop on Deep Learning for Speech Recognition and Related Applications*.

Frederic Morin and Yoshua Bengio. 2005. Hierarchical probabilistic neural network language model. In *Proc. AISTATS05*, pages 246–252.

Douglas B. Paul and Janet M. Baker. 1992. The design for the wall street journal-based csr corpus. In *Proc. DARPA Speech and Natural Language Workshop*, page 357362.

Tara N. Sainath, Brian Kingsbury, and Bhuvana Ramabhadran. 2012. Improvements in Using Deep Belief Networks for Large Vocabulary Continuous Speech Recognition. Technical report, IBM, Speech and Language Algorithms Group.

Ruhi Sarikaya, Mohamed Afify, and Brian Kingsbury. 2009. Tied-mixture language modeling in continuous space. In *HLT-NAACL*, pages 459–467.

Holger Schwenk and Jean-Luc Gauvain. 2005. Training neural network language models on very large corpora. In *Proc. HLT-EMNLP 2005*, pages 201–208.

Holger Schwenk. 2007. Continuous space language models. *Comput. Speech Lang.*, 21(3):492–518, July.

Frank Seide, Gang Li, Xie Chen, and Dong Yu. 2011. Feature Engineering in Context-Dependent Deep Neural Networks for Conversational Speech Transcription. In *Proc. ASRU*.

Hagen Soltau, George. Saon, and Brian Kingsbury. 2010. The IBM Attila speech recognition toolkit. In *Proc. IEEE Workshop on Spoken Language Technology*, pages 97–102.

Hai Son Le, Ilya Oparin, Alexandre Allauzen, Jean-Luc Gauvain, and Francois Yvon. 2011. Structured output layer neural network language model. In *Proceedings of IEEE International Conference on Acoustic, Speech and Signal Processing*, pages 5524–5527, Prague, Czech Republic.

Andreas Stolcke. 1998. Entropy-based pruning of backoff language models. In *Proceedings of DARPA Broadcast News Transcription and Understanding Workshop*, pages 270 – 274, Lansdowne, VA, USA.

A Challenge Set for Advancing Language Modeling

Geoffrey Zweig and Chris J.C. Burges
Microsoft Research
Redmond, WA 98052

Abstract

In this paper, we describe a new, publicly available corpus intended to stimulate research into language modeling techniques which are sensitive to overall sentence coherence. The task uses the Scholastic Aptitude Test's sentence completion format. The test set consists of 1040 sentences, each of which is missing a content word. The goal is to select the correct replacement from amongst five alternates. In general, all of the options are syntactically valid, and reasonable with respect to local N-gram statistics. The set was generated by using an N-gram language model to generate a long list of likely words, given the immediate context. These options were then hand-groomed, to identify four decoys which are globally incoherent, yet syntactically correct. To ensure the right to public distribution, all the data is derived from out-of-copyright materials from Project Gutenberg. The test sentences were derived from five of Conan Doyle's Sherlock Holmes novels, and we provide a large set of Nineteenth and early Twentieth Century texts as training material.

1 Introduction

Perhaps beginning with Claude Shannon's use of N-gram statistics to compute the perplexity of letter sequences (Shannon and Weaver, 1949), N-gram models have grown to be the most commonly used type of language model in human language technologies. At the word level, N-gram modeling techniques have been extensively refined, with state-of-the-art techniques based on smoothed N-gram counts (Kneser and Ney, 1995; Chen and Goodman, 1999), multi-layer perceptrons (Schwenk and Gauvain, 2002; Schwenk, 2007) and maximum-entropy models (Rosenfeld, 1997; Chen, 2009a; Chen, 2009b). Trained on large amounts of data, these methods have proven very effective in both speech recognition and machine translation applications.

Concurrent with the refinement of N-gram modeling techniques, there has been an important stream of research focused on the incorporation of syntactic and semantic information (Chelba and Jelinek, 1998; Chelba and Jelinek, 2000; Rosenfeld et al., 2001; Yamada and Knight, 2001; Khudanpur and Wu, 2000; Wu and Khudanpur, 1999). Since intuitively, language is about expressing *meaning* in a highly structured syntactic form, it has come as something of a surprise that the improvements from these methods have been modest, and the methods have yet to be widely adopted in non-research systems.

One explanation for this is that the tasks to which language modeling has been most extensively applied are largely soluble with local information. In the speech recognition application, there is a fundamental confluence of acoustic and linguistic information, and the language model can be thought of as resolving ambiguity only between acoustically confusable words (Printz and Olsen, 2002). Since words which are acoustically similar, e.g. "bill" and "spill" usually appear in very different textual contexts, the local information of an N-gram language model may be adequate to distinguish them. To a lesser degree, in a machine translation application,

1. One of the characters in Milton Murayama's novel is considered _______ because he deliberately defies an oppressive hierarchical society.
(A) rebellious (B) impulsive (C) artistic (D) industrious (E) tyrannical

2. Whether substances are medicines or poisons often depends on dosage, for substances that are ________ in small doses can be _______ in large.
(A) useless .. effective
(B) mild .. benign
(C) curative .. toxic
(D) harmful .. fatal
(E) beneficial .. miraculous

Figure 1: Sample sentence completion questions (Educational-Testing-Service, 2011).

the potential phrase translations may be similar in meaning and local information may again suffice to make a good selection.

In this paper, we present a language processing corpus which has been explicitly designed to be non-solvable using purely N-gram based methods, and which instead requires some level of semantic processing. To do this, we draw inspiration from the standardized testing paradigm, and propose a *sentence completion* task along the lines of that found in the widely used Scholastic Aptitude Test. In this type of question, one is given a sentence with one or two words removed, and asked to select from among a set of five possible insertions. Two examples of SAT test questions are shown in Figure 1.

As can be seen, the options available all make sense from the local N-gram point of view, and are all syntactically valid; only semantic considerations allow the correct answer to be distinguished. We believe this sort of question is useful for two key reasons: first, its full solution will require language modeling techniques which are qualitatively different than N-grams; and secondly, the basic task formulation has been externally determined and is a widely used method for assessing human abilities. Unfortunately, to date no publicly available corpus of such questions has been released.

The contribution of this work is to release a public corpus of sentence completion questions designed to stimulate research in language modeling technology which moves beyond N-grams to explicitly address global sentence coherence. The corpus is based purely on out-of-copyright data from Project Gutenberg, thus allowing us to distribute it. The test questions consist of sentences taken from five Sherlock Holmes novels. In each, a word has been removed, and the task is to choose from among five alternatives. One of the options is the original word, and the other four "decoys" have been generated from an N-gram language model using local context. Sampling from an N-gram model is done to generate alternates which make sense locally, but for which there is no other reason to expect them to make sense globally. To ensure that synonyms of the correct answer are not present, and that the options are syntactically reasonable, the decoys have been hand selected from among a large number of possibilities suggested by the N-gram model. The training data consists of approximately 500 out-of-copyright Nineteenth and early Twentieth century novels, also from Project Gutenberg.

We expect that the successful development of models of global coherence will be useful in a variety of tasks, including:

- the interactive generation of sentence completion questions for vocabulary tutoring applications;
- proof-reading;
- automated grading of essays and other student work; and
- sentence generation in free-form dialog applications.

The remainder of this paper is organized as follows. In Section 2, we describe the process by which we made the corpus. Section 3 provides guidance as to the proper use of the data. In Section 4, we present baseline results using several simple automated methods for answering the questions. Finally, in Section 5, we discuss related work.

2 The Question Generation Process

Question generation was done in two steps. First, a candidate sentence containing an infrequent word was selected, and alternates for that word were automatically determined by sampling with an N-gram language model. The N-gram model used the immediate history as context, thus resulting in words that may "look good" locally, but for which there is no a-priori reason to expect them to make sense globally. In the second step, we eliminated choices which are obviously incorrect because they constitute grammatical errors. Choices requiring semantic knowledge and logical inference were preferred, as described in the guidelines, which we give in Section 3. Note that an important *desideratum* guiding the data generation process was requiring that a researcher who knows exactly how the data was created, including knowing which data was used to train the language model, should nevertheless not be able to use that information to solve the problem. We now describe the data that was used, and then describe the two steps in more detail.

2.1 Data Used

Seed sentences were selected from five of Conan Doyle's Sherlock Holmes novels: *The Sign of Four (1890), The Hound of the Baskervilles (1892), The Adventures of Sherlock Holmes (1892), The Memoirs of Sherlock Holmes (1894),* and *The Valley of Fear (1915).* Once a *focus word* within the sentence was selected, alternates to that word were generated using an N-gram language model. This model was trained on approximately 540 texts from the Project Gutenberg collection, consisting mainly of 19th century novels. Of these 522 had adequate headers attesting to lack of copyright, and they are now available at the *Sentence Completion Challenge* website `http://research.microsoft.com/en-us/projects/scc/`.

2.2 Automatically Generating Alternates

Alternates were generated for every sentence containing an infrequent word. A state-of-the-art class-based maximum entropy N-gram model (Chen, 2009b) was used to generate the alternates. Ideally, these alternates would be generated according to $P(\text{alternate}|\text{remainder of sentence})$. This can be done by computing the probability of the completed sentence once for every possible vocabulary word, and then normalizing and sampling. However, the normalization over all words is computationally expensive, and we have used a procedure based on sampling based on the preceding two word history only, and then re-ordering based on a larger context. The following procedure was used:

1. Select a *focus word* with overall frequency less than 10^{-4}. For example, we might select "extraordinary" in "It is really the most extraordinary and inexplicable business."

2. Use the two-word history immediately preceding the selected focus word to predict alternates. We sampled 150 unique alternates at this stage, requiring that they all have frequency less than 10^{-4}. For example, "the most" predicts "handsome" and "luminous."

3. If the original (correct) sentence has a better score than any of these alternates, reject the sentence.

4. Else, score each option according to how well it and its immediate predecessor predict the next word. For example, the probability of "and" following "most handsome" might be 0.012.

5. Sort the predicted words according to this score, and retain the top 30 options.

In step 3, omitting questions for which the correct sentence is the best makes the set of options more difficult to solve with a language model alone. However, by allowing the correct sentence to potentially fall below the set of alternates retained, an opposite bias is created: the language model will tend to assign a lower score to the correct option than to the alternates (which were chosen by virtue of scoring well). We measured the bias by performing a test on the 1,040 test sentences using the language model, and choosing the *lowest* scoring candidate as the answer. This gave an accuracy of 26% (as opposed to 31%, found by taking the highest scoring candidate: recall that a random choice would give 20% in expectation). Thus although there is some remaining bias for the answer to be low scoring, it is small. When a language model other than the precise one used to generate the data is used, the score reversal test yielded 17% correct. The correct polarity gave 39%. If, however, just the single score used to do the sort in the last step is used (i.e. the probability of the immediate successor alone), then the lowest scoring alternate is correct about 38% of the time - almost as much as the language model itself. The use of the word score occurring two positions after the focus also achieves 38%, though a positive polarity is beneficial here. Combined, these scores achieve about 43%. Neither is anywhere close to human performance. We are currently evaluating a second round of test questions, in which we still sample options based on the preceding history, but re-order them according the the total sentence probability $P(w_1 \ldots w_N)$.

The overall procedure has the effect of providing options which are both well-predicted by the immediate history, and predictive of the immediate future. Since in total the procedure uses just four consecutive words, it cannot be expected to provide globally coherent alternates. However, sometimes it does produce synonyms to the correct word, as well as syntactically invalid options, which must be weeded out. For this, we examine the alternates by hand.

2.3 Human Grooming

The human judges picked the best four choices of impostor sentences from the automatically generated list of thirty, and were given the following instructions:

1. All chosen sentences should be grammatically correct. For example: *He dances while he ate his pipe* would be illegal.

2. Each correct answer should be unambiguous. In other words, the correct answer should always be a significantly better fit for that sentence than each of the four impostors; it should be possible to write down an explanation as to why the correct answer is the correct answer, that would persuade most reasonable people.

3. Sentences that might cause offense or controversy should be avoided.

4. Ideally the alternatives will require some thought in order to determine the correct answer. For example:

   - *Was she his [client | musings | discomfiture | choice | opportunity] , his friend , or his mistress?*

   would constitute a good test sentence. In order to arrive at the correct answer, the student must notice that, while *"musings"* and *"discomfiture"* are both clearly wrong, the terms *friend* and *mistress* both describe people, which therefore makes *client* a more likely choice than *choice* or *opportunity*.

5. Alternatives that require understanding properties of entities that are mentioned in the sentence are desirable. For example:

   - *All red-headed men who are above the age of [800 | seven | twenty-one | 1,200 | 60,000] years , are eligible.*

   requires that the student realize that a *man* cannot be seven years old, or 800 or more. However, such examples are rare: most often, arriving at the answer will require thought, but not detailed entity knowledge, such as:

   - *That is his [generous | mother's | successful | favorite | main] fault , but on the whole he's a good worker.*

6. Dictionary use is encouraged, if necessary.

7. A given sentence from the set of five novels should only be used once. If more than one focus word has been identified for a sentence (i.e. different focuses have been identified, in different positions), choose the set of sentences that generates the best challenge, according to the above guidelines.

Note that the impostors sometimes constitute a perfectly fine completion, but that in those cases, the correct completion is still clearly identifiable as the most likely completion.

2.4 Sample Questions

Figure 2 shows ten examples of the Holmes derived questions. The full set is available at `http://research.microsoft.com/en-us/projects/scc/`.

3 Guidelines for Use

It is important for users of this data to realize the following: since the test data was taken from five 19th century novels, the test data itself is likely to occur in

1) I have seen it on him , and could _____ to it.
a) write b) migrate c) climb d) swear e) contribute

2) They seize him and use violence towards him in order to make him sign some papers to make over the girl's _____ of which he may be trustee to them.
a) appreciation b) activity c) suspicions d) administration e) fortune

3) My morning's work has not been _____ , since it has proved that he has the very strongest motives for standing in the way of anything of the sort.
a) invisible b) neglected c) overlooked d) wasted e) deliberate

4) It was furred outside by a thick layer of dust , and damp and worms had eaten through the wood , so that a crop of livid fungi was _____ on the inside of it.
a) sleeping b) running c) resounding d) beheaded e) growing

5) Presently he emerged , looking even more _____ than before.
a) instructive b) reassuring c) unprofitable d) flurried e) numerous

6) We took no _____ to hide it.
a) fault b) instructions c) permission d) pains e) fidelity

7) I stared at it _____ , not knowing what was about to issue from it.
a) afterwards b) rapidly c) forever d) horror-stricken e) lightly

8) The probability was , therefore , that she was _____ the truth , or , at least , a part of the truth.
a) addressing b) telling c) selling d) surveying e) undergoing

9) The furniture was scattered about in every direction , with dismantled shelves and open drawers , as if the lady had hurriedly _____ them before her flight.
a) warned b) rebuked c) assigned d) ransacked e) taught

10) The sun had set and _____ was settling over the moor.
a) dusk b) mischief c) success d) disappointment e) laughter

Figure 2: The first ten questions from the Holmes Corpus.

the index of most Web search engines, and in other large scale data-sets that were constructed from web data (for example, the Google N-gram project). For example, entering the string *That is his fault , but on the whole he's a good worker* (one of the sentence examples given above, but with the focus word removed) into the Bing search engine results in the correct (full) sentence at the top position. It is important to realize that researchers may inadvertently get better results than truly warranted because they have used data that is thus tainted by the test set. To help prevent any such criticism from being leveled at a particular publication, we recommend than in any set of published results, the exact data used for training and validation be specified. The training data provided on our website may also be considered "safe" and useful for making comparisons across sites.

4 Baseline Results

4.1 A Simple 4-gram model

As a sanity check we constructed a very simple N-gram model as follows: given a test sentence (with the position of the focus word known), the score for that sentence was initialized to zero, and then incremented by one for each bigram match, by two for each trigram match, and by three for each 4-gram match, where a match means that the N-gram in the test sentence containing the focus word occurs at least once in the background data. This simple method achieved 34% correct (compared to 20% by random choice) on the test set.

4.2 Smoothed N-gram model

As a somewhat more sophisticated baseline, we use the CMU language modeling toolkit [1] to build a 4-gram language model using Good-Turing smoothing. We kept all bigrams and trigrams occurring in the data, as well as four-grams occurring at least twice. We used a vocabulary of the 126k words that occurred five or more times, resulting in a total of 26M N-grams. Sentences were ordered according to their probability according to the language model: $P(w_1 \ldots w_N)$. This improved by 5% absolute on the simple baseline to achieve 39% correct.

4.3 Latent Semantic Analysis Similarity

As a final benchmark, we present scores for a novel method based on latent semantic analysis. In this approach, we treated each sentence in the training data as a "document" and performed latent semantic analysis (Deerwester et al., 1990) to obtain a 300 dimensional vector representation of each word in the vocabulary. Denoting two words by their vectors $\mathbf{x}, \mathbf{y}$, their similarity is defined as the cosine of the angle between them:

$$\mathtt{sim}(\mathbf{x}, \mathbf{y}) = \frac{\mathbf{x} \cdot \mathbf{y}}{\parallel \mathbf{x} \parallel \parallel \mathbf{y} \parallel}.$$

To decide which option to select, we computed the average similarity to every other word in the sentence, and then output the word with the greatest overall similarity. This results in our best baseline performance, at 49% correct.

4.4 Benchmark Summary

Table 1 summarizes our benchmark study. First, for reference, we had an unaffiliated human answer a random subset of 100 questions. Ninety-one percent were answered correctly, showing that scores in the range of 90% are reasonable to expect. Secondly, we tested the performance of the same model (Model M) that was used to generate the data. Because this model output alternates that it assigns high-probability, there is a bias against it, and it scored 31%. Smoothed 3 and 4-gram models built with the CMU toolkit achieved 36 to 39 percent. Recall that the sampling process introduced some bias into the word scores at specific positions relative to the focus word. Exploiting the negative bias induced on the immediately following word, and combining it with the score of the word two positions in the future, we were able to obtain 43%. The simple 4-gram model described earlier did somewhat worse than the other N-gram language models, and the LSA similarity model did best with 49%. As a further check on this data, we have run the same tests on 108 sentence completion questions from a practice SAT exam (Princeton Review, *11 Practice Tests for the SAT & PSAT*, 2011 Edition). To train language models for the SAT question task, we used 1.2 billion words of Los Angeles Times data taken from the years 1985 through 2002. Results for the SAT data are similar, with N-gram language models scoring 42-44% depending on vocabulary size and smoothing, and LSA similarity attaining 46%.

Method	**% Correct** (N=1040)
Human	91
Generating Model	31
Smoothed 3-gram	36
Smoothed 4-gram	39
Positional combination	43
Simple 4-gram	34
Average LSA Similarity	49

Table 1: Summary of Benchmarks

These results indicate that the "Holmes" sentence completion set is indeed a challenging problem, and has a level of difficulty roughly comparable to that of SAT questions. Simple models based on N-gram statistics do quite poorly, and even a relatively sophisticated semantic-coherence model struggles to beat the 50% mark.

5 Related Work

The past work which is most similar to ours is derived from the lexical substitution track of SemEval-2007 (McCarthy and Navigli, 2007). In this task, the challenge is to find a replacement for a word or

[1] *http://www.speech.cs.cmu.edu/SLM/toolkit.html*

phrase removed from a sentence. In contrast to our SAT-inspired task, the original answer is indicated. For example, one might be asked to find replacements for *match* in "After the *match*, replace any remaining fluid deficit to prevent problems of chronic dehydration throughout the tournament." Scoring is done by comparing a system's results with those produced by a group of human annotators (not unlike the use of multiple translations in machine translation). Several forms of scoring are defined using formulae which make the results impossible to compare with correct/incorrect multiple choice scoring. Under the provided scoring metrics, two consistently high-performing systems in the SemEval 2007 evaluations are the KU (Yuret, 2007) and UNT (Hassan et al., 2007) systems. These operate in two phases: first they find a set of potential replacement words, and then they rank them. The KU system uses just an N-gram language model to do this ranking. The UNT system uses a large variety of information sources, each with a different weight. A language model is used, and this receives the highest weight. N-gram statistics were also very effective - according to one of the scoring paradigms - in (Giuliano et al., 2007); as a separate entry, this paper further explored the use of Latent Semantic Analysis to measure the degree of similarity between a potential replacement and its context, but the results were poorer than others. Since the original word provides a strong hint as to the possible meanings of the replacements, we hypothesize that N-gram statistics are largely able to resolve the remaining ambiguities, thus accounting for the good performance of these methods on this task. The Holmes data does not have this property and thus may be more challenging.

ESL synonym questions were studied by Turney (2001), and subsequently considered by numerous research groups including Terra and Clarke (2003) and Pado and Lapata (2007). These questions are easier than the SemEval task because in addition to the original word and the sentence context, the list of options is provided. For example, one might be asked to identify a replacement for "rusty" in "A [rusty] nail is not as strong as a clean, new one. *(corroded; black; dirty; painted).*" Jarmasz and Szpakowicz (2003) used a sophisticated thesaurus-based method and achieved state-of-the art performance on the ESL synonyms task, which is 82%. Again the Holmes data does not have the property that the intended meaning is signaled by providing the original word, thus adding extra challenge.

Although it was not developed for this task, we believe the recurrent language modeling work of Mikolov (2010; 2011b; 2011a) is also quite relevant. In this work, a recurrent neural net language model is used to achieve state-of-the-art performance in perplexity and speech recognition error rates. Critically, the recurrent neural net does not maintain a fixed N-gram context, and its hidden layer has the potential to model overall sentence meaning and long-span coherence. While theoretical results (Bengio et al., 1994) indicate that extremely long-range phenomena are hard to learn with a recurrent neural network, in practice the span of usual sentences may be manageable. Recursive neural networks (Socher et al., 2011) offer similar advantages, without the theoretical limitations. Both offer promising avenues of research.

6 Conclusion

In this paper we have described a new, publicly available, corpus of sentence-completion questions. Whereas for many traditional language modeling tasks, N-gram models provide state-of-the-art performance, and may even be fully adequate, this task is designed to be insoluble with local models. Because the task now allows us to measure progress in an area where N-gram models do poorly, we expect it to stimulate research in fundamentally new and more powerful language modeling methods.

References

Yoshua Bengio, Patrice Simard, and Paolo Frasconi. 1994. Learning long-term dependencies with gradient descent is difficult. *IEEE Transactions on Neural Networks*, 5(2):157 –166.

Ciprian Chelba and Frederick Jelinek. 1998. Exploiting syntactic structure for language modeling. In *Proceedings of the 36th Annual Meeting of the Association for Computational Linguistics and 17th International Conference on Computational Linguistics - Volume 1*, ACL '98, pages 225–231, Stroudsburg, PA, USA. Association for Computational Linguistics.

Ciprian Chelba and Frederick Jelinek. 2000. Structured

language modeling. *Computer Speech and Language*, 14(4):283 – 332.

Stanley F. Chen and Joshua Goodman. 1999. An empirical study of smoothing techniques for language modeling. *Computer Speech and Language*, 13(4):359 – 393.

S. Chen. 2009a. Performance prediction for exponential language models. In *NAACL-HLT*.

S. Chen. 2009b. Shrinking exponential language models. In *NAACL-HLT*.

S. Deerwester, S.T. Dumais, G.W. Furnas, T.K. Landauer, and R. Harshman. 1990. Indexing by latent semantic analysis. *Journal of the American Society for Information Science*, 41(96).

Educational-Testing-Service. 2011. https://satonlinecourse.collegeboard.com/sr/ digital_assets/assessment/pdf/0833a611-0a43-10c2-0148-cc8c0087fb06-f.pdf.

Claudio Giuliano, Alfio Gliozzo, and Carlo Strapparava. 2007. Fbk-irst: Lexical substitution task exploiting domain and syntagmatic coherence. In *Proceedings of the 4th International Workshop on Semantic Evaluations*, SemEval '07, pages 145–148, Stroudsburg, PA, USA. Association for Computational Linguistics.

Samer Hassan, Andras Csomai, Carmen Banea, Ravi Sinha, and Rada Mihalcea. 2007. Unt: Subfinder: Combining knowledge sources for automatic lexical substitution. In *Proceedings of the 4th International Workshop on Semantic Evaluations*, SemEval '07, pages 410–413, Stroudsburg, PA, USA. Association for Computational Linguistics.

Sanjeev Khudanpur and Jun Wu. 2000. Maximum entropy techniques for exploiting syntactic, semantic and collocational dependencies in language modeling. *Computer Speech and Language*, 14(4):355 – 372.

R. Kneser and H. Ney. 1995. Improved backing-off for m-gram language modeling. In *Proceedings of ICASSP*.

Jarmasz M. and Szpakowicz S. 2003. Roget's thesaurus and semantic similarity. In *Recent Advances in Natural Language Processing (RANLP)*.

Diana McCarthy and Roberto Navigli. 2007. Semeval-2007 task 10: English lexical substitution task. In *Proceedings of the 4th International Workshop on Semantic Evaluations (SemEval-2007)*, pages 48–53.

Tomas Mikolov, Martin Karafiat, Jan Cernocky, and Sanjeev Khudanpur. 2010. Recurrent neural network based language model. In *Proceedings of Interspeech 2010*.

Tomas Mikolov, Anoop Deoras, Stefan Kombrink, Lukas Burget, and Jan Cernocky. 2011a. Empirical evaluation and combination of advanced language modeling techniques. In *Proceedings of Interspeech 2011*.

Tomas Mikolov, Stefan Kombrink, Lukas Burget, Jan Cernocky, and Sanjeev Khudanpur. 2011b. Extensions of recurrent neural network based language model. In *Proceedings of ICASSP 2011*.

Sebastian Pado and Mirella Lapata. 2007. Dependency-based construction of semantic space models. *Computational Linguistics, 33 (2)*, pages 161–199.

Harry Printz and Peder A. Olsen. 2002. Theory and practice of acoustic confusability. *Computer Speech and Language*, 16(1):131 – 164.

Ronald Rosenfeld, Stanley F. Chen, and Xiaojin Zhu. 2001. Whole-sentence exponential language models: a vehicle for linguistic-statistical integration. *Computer Speech and Language*, 15(1):55 – 73.

R. Rosenfeld. 1997. A whole sentence maximum entropy language model. In *Proceedings ASRU*.

Holger Schwenk and Jean-Luc Gauvain. 2002. Connectionist language modeling for large vocabulary continuous speech recognition. In *Proceedings of ICASSP*.

Holger Schwenk. 2007. Continuous space language models. *Computer Speech and Language*, 21(3):492 – 518.

Claude E. Shannon and Warren Weaver. 1949. *The Mathematical Theory of Communication*. University of Illinois Press.

Richard Socher, Cliff Chiung-Yu Lin, Andrew Y. Ng, and Christopher D. Manning. 2011. Parsing natural scenes and natural language with recursive neural networks. In *Proceedings of the 2011 International Conference on Machine Learning (ICML-2011)*.

E. Terra and C. Clarke. 2003. Frequency estimates for statistical word similarity measures. In *Conference of the North American Chapter of the Association for Computational Linguistics (NAACL)*.

Peter D. Turney. 2001. Mining the web for synonyms: PMI-IR versus LSA on TOEFL. In *European Conference on Machine Learning (ECML)*.

Jun Wu and Sanjeev Khudanpur. 1999. Combining non-local, syntactic and n-gram dependencies in language modeling. In *Proceedings of Eurospeech*.

Kenji Yamada and Kevin Knight. 2001. A syntax-based statistical translation model. In *Proceedings of the 39th Annual Meeting on Association for Computational Linguistics*, ACL '01, pages 523–530, Stroudsburg, PA, USA. Association for Computational Linguistics.

Deniz Yuret. 2007. Ku: word sense disambiguation by substitution. In *Proceedings of the 4th International Workshop on Semantic Evaluations*, SemEval '07, pages 207–213, Stroudsburg, PA, USA. Association for Computational Linguistics.

Unsupervised Vocabulary Adaptation for Morph-based Language Models

André Mansikkaniemi and **Mikko Kurimo**
Aalto University School of Science
Department of Information and Computer Science
PO BOX 15400, 00076 Aalto, Finland
{andre.mansikkaniemi,mikko.kurimo}@aalto.fi

Abstract

Modeling of foreign entity names is an important unsolved problem in morpheme-based modeling that is common in morphologically rich languages. In this paper we present an unsupervised vocabulary adaptation method for morph-based speech recognition. Foreign word candidates are detected automatically from in-domain text through the use of letter n-gram perplexity. Over-segmented foreign entity names are restored to their base forms in the morph-segmented in-domain text for easier and more reliable modeling and recognition. The adapted pronunciation rules are finally generated with a trainable grapheme-to-phoneme converter. In ASR performance the unsupervised method almost matches the ability of supervised adaptation in correctly recognizing foreign entity names.

1 Introduction

Foreign entity names (FENs) are difficult to recognize correctly in automatic speech recognition (ASR). Pronunciation rules that cover native words usually give incorrect pronunciation for foreign words. More often the foreign entity names encountered in speech are out-of-vocabulary words, previously unseen words not present in neither the lexicon nor background language model (LM).

An in-domain LM trained on a smaller corpus related to the topic of the speech, can be used to adapt the background LM to give more suitable probabilities to rare or unseen foreign words. Proper pronunciation rules for foreign entity names are needed to increase the probability of their correct recognition. These can either be obtained from a hand-made lexicon or by generating pronunciation rules automatically using for example a trainable grapheme-to-phoneme (G2P) converter.

In morph-based speech recognition words are segmented into sub-word units called morphemes. When using statistical morph-segmentation algorithms such as Morfessor (Creutz and Lagus, 2005) new foreign entity names encountered in in-domain text corpora are often over-segmented (e.g. mcdowell ⇒ mc do well). To guarantee reliable pronunciation modeling, it's preferable to keep the lemma intact. Restoring over-segmented foreign entity names back in to their base forms is referred to as morpheme adaptation in this paper.

This work describes an unsupervised approach to language and pronunciation modeling of foreign entity names in morph-based speech recognition. We will study an adaptation framework illustrated below in Figure 1.

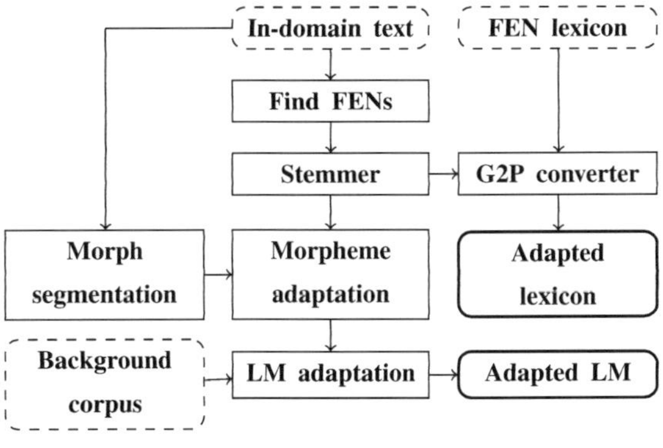

Figure 1: Adaptation framework.

The adaptation framework is centered around the following automated steps: 1. Find foreign words in adaptation texts, 2. Convert foreign word candidates into their base forms, 3. Generate pronunciation variants for the retrieved foreign entity name candidates using a G2P converter. Additionally, to facilitate easier and more reliable pronunciation adaptation, the foreign entity names are restored to their base forms in the segmented in-domain text.

The adaptation framework will be compared to a supervised method where the adaptation steps are done manually. The evaluation will be done on Finnish radio news segments.

2 Methods

2.1 Foreign Word Detection

Unsupervised detection of foreign words in text has previously been implemented for English using word n-ngram models (Ahmed, 2005).

Finnish has a rich morphology and using word n-gram models or dictionaries for the detection of foreign words would not be practical. Many of the foreign words occurring in written Finnish texts could be identified from unusual letter sequences that are not common in native words. A letter n-gram model trained on Finnish words could be used to identify foreign words by calculating the average perplexity of the letter sequence in a word normalized by its length.

A two-step algorithm is implemented for the automatic detection of foreign words. First, all words starting in uppercase letters in the unprocessed adaptation text are held out as potential foreign entity names. The perplexity for each foreign word candidate is calculated using a letter-ngram model trained on Finnish words. Words with the highest perplexity values are the most probable foreign entity names. A percentage threshold T for the top perplexity words can be determined from prior information.

The most likely foreign words are finally converted into their base forms using a Finnish stemming algorithm (*Snowball* - `http://snowball.tartarus.org/`).

2.2 Lexicon Adaptation

For Finnish ASR systems the pronunciation dictionary can easily be constructed for arbitrary words by mapping letters directly to phonemes. Foreign names are often pronounced according to their original languages, which can have more complicated pronunciation rules. These pronunciation rules can either be manually added to a lookup dictionary or generated automatically with a grapheme-to-phoneme converter. Constructing a foreign word lexicon through manual input involves a lot of tedious work and it will require a continuous effort to keep it updated.

In this work *Sequitur G2P* is used, a data-driven grapheme-to-phoneme converter based on joint-sequence models (Bisani and Ney, 2008). A pronunciation model is trained on a manually constructed foreign word lexicon consisting of 2000 foreign entity names with a manually given pronunciation hand-picked from a Finnish newswire text collection. The linguistic origins of the foreign words are mixed but Germanic and Slavic languages are the most common.

The pronunciation model is used to generate the most probable pronunciation variants for the foreign entity name candidates found in the adaptation text.

2.3 Morpheme Adaptation

In current state of the art Finnish language modeling words are segmented into sub-word units (morphemes) (Hirsimäki et. al, 2009). This allows the system to cover a large number of words which result from the highly agglutinative word morphology.

Over-segmentation usually occurs for previously unseen words found in adaptation texts. To ensure reliable pronunciation modeling of foreign entity names it's preferable to keep the lemma intact. Mapping a whole word pronunciation rule onto separate morphemes is a non-trivial task for non-phonetic languages such as English. The morphemes in the in-domain corpus will be adapted such that all foreign words are restored into their base forms and the base forms are added to the morpheme vocabulary. Below is an example. Word boundaries are labeled with the <*w*>-tag.

<*w*> ***oilers*** <*w*> *hävisi* <*w*> ***edmonton*** *in* <*w*> ***com mon we al th*** <*w*> ***sta dium*** *illa* <*w*>

$\Rightarrow$

<*w*> ***oilers*** <*w*> *hävisi* <*w*> ***edmonton*** *in* <*w*> ***commonwealth*** <*w*> ***stadium*** *illa* <*w*>

2.4 Language Model Adaptation

The in-domain adaptation text is segmented differently depending on the foreign entity name candidates that are included. A separate in-domain LM $P_i(w|h)$ is trained for each segmentation of the text. Linear interpolation is used to the adapt the background LM $P_B(w|h)$ with the in-domain LM $P_i(w|h)$.

$$P_{adap_i}(w|h) = \lambda P_i(w|h) + (1 - \lambda)P_B(w|h) \qquad (1)$$

3 Experiments

3.1 Speech Data

Evaluation data consisted of two sets of Finnish radio news segments in 16 kHz audio. All of the recordings were collected in 2011-2012 from YLE Radio Suomi news and sports programs.

The first data set consisted of 32 general news segments. The total transcription length was 8271 words. 4.8% of the words were categorized as foreign entity names (FEN). The second data set consisted of 43 sports news segments. The total transcription length 6466 was words. 7.9% of the words were categorized as foreign entity names.

3.2 System and Models

All speech recognition experiments were run on the Aalto speech recognizer (Hirsimäki et. al, 2009).

The background LM was trained on the Kielipankki corpus (70 million words). A lexicon of 30k morphs and a model of morph segmentation was learnt from the same corpus as the LM using Morfessor (Creutz and Lagus, 2005). The baseline lexicon was adapted with a manually transcribed pronunciation dictionary of 2000 foreign entity names found in Finnish newswire texts. A Kneser-Ney smoothed varigram LM (n=12) was trained on the segmented corpus with the variKN language modeling toolkit (Siivola et al., 2007).

LM adaptation data was manually collected from the Web. On average 2-3 articles were gathered per topic featured in the evaluation data sets. 120 000 words of text were gathered for LM adaptation on the general news set. 60 000 words were gathered for LM adaptation on the sports news set.

The foreign word detection algorithm and a letter trigram model trained on the Kielipankki word list were used to automatically find foreign entity names in the adaptation texts and convert them into their base forms. Different values were used as percentage threshold T (30, 60, and 100%).

The adaptation texts were segmented into morphs with the segmentation model learnt from the background corpus. Morpheme adaptation was performed by restoring the foreign entity name candidates into their base forms. Separate in-domain varigram LMs (n=6) were trained for adaptation data segmented into morphs using each choice of T in the foreign name detection. The background LM was adapted with each in-domain LM separately using linear interpolation with weight $\lambda = 0.1$ chosen based on preliminary experiments.

A pronunciation model was trained with *Sequitur G2P* on the manually constructed foreign word lexicon. The number of the most probable pronunciation variants m for one word to be used in lexicon adaptation, was tested with different values (1, 4, and 8).

4 Results

The word error rate (WER), letter error rate (LER), and the foreign entity name error rate (FENER) are reported in the results. All the results are presented in Table 1.

The first experiment was run on the baseline system. The average WER is 21.7% for general news and 34.0% for sports. The average FENER is significantly higher for both (76.6% and 80.7%).

Supervised vocabulary adaptation was implemented by manually retrieving the foreign entity names from the adaptation text and adding their pronunciation rules to the lexicon. Morpheme adaptation was also applied. Compared to only using linear interpolation ($\lambda = 0.1$) supervised vocabulary adaptation reduces WER by 4% (general news) and 6% (sports news). Recognition of foreign entity names is also improved with FENER reductions of 18% and 24%.

Unsupervised vocabulary adaptation was implemented through automatic retrieval and pronunciation generation of foreign entity names. The parameters of interest are the foreign name percentage threshold T, determining how many foreign word candidates are included for lexicon and morpheme adaptation and m, the number of pronunciation vari-

Adaptation method				Results					
LM	Lexicon			General News			Sports News		
	Adaptation	*T*[%]	*m*	WER[%]	LER[%]	FENER[%]	WER[%]	LER[%]	FENER[%]
Background	Baseline			21.7	5.7	76.6	34.0	11.4	80.7
Background + Adaptation	Baseline			20.6	5.3	67.8	32.0	10.7	69.4
	Supervised	-	1	**19.8**	**5.0**	**55.7**	**30.1**	**9.8**	**53.1**
	Unsupervised	30	1	20.4	5.2	64.0	31.5	10.4	64.1
			4	**20.2**	**5.2**	58.7	31.6	10.4	60.4
			8	20.4	5.3	**56.9**	31.5	10.4	56.8
		60	1	20.7	5.3	63.7	32.3	10.4	63.7
			4	20.7	5.3	59.4	31.1	9.9	59.8
			8	21.1	5.5	58.2	**31.0**	**9.9**	**55.6**
		100	1	21.1	5.4	62.7	33.2	10.7	66.1
			4	21.2	5.5	58.2	32.6	10.4	60.7
			8	22.1	5.9	59.2	33.2	10.6	57.0

Table 1: Results of adaptation experiments on the two test sets. Linear interpolation is tested with supervised and unsupervised vocabulary adaptation. T is the top percentage of foreign entity name candidates used in unsupervised vocabulary adaptation, and m is the number of pronunciation variants for each word.

ants generated for each word. The best performance is reached on the general news set with $T = 30\%$ and $m = 4$ (WER = 20.2%, FENER = 58.7%), and on the sports news set with $T = 60\%$ and $m = 8$ (WER = 31.0%, FENER = 55.6%).

5 Conclusion and Discussion

In this work we presented an unsupervised approach to pronunciation and language modeling of foreign entity names in morph-based speech recognition.

In the context of LM adaptation, foreign entity name candidates were retrieved from in-domain texts using a foreign word detection algorithm. Pronunciation variants were generated for the foreign word candidates using a grapheme-to-phoneme converter. Morpheme adaptation was also applied by restoring the foreign entity names into their base forms in the morph-segmented adaptation texts.

The results indicate that unsupervised pronunciation and language modeling of foreign entity names is feasible. The unsupervised approach almost matches supervised adaptation in correctly recognizing foreign entity names. Average WER is also very close to the supervised adaptation one despite the increased acoustic confusability when introducing more pronunciation variants. The percentage of foreign word candidates included for adaptation affects performance of the algorithm. Including all words starting in uppercase letters significantly degrades ASR results. The optimal threshold value is dependent on the adaptation text and its foreign word frequency and similarity to the evaluation data.

The composition of likely pronunciations of foreign names by Finnish speakers is not a straightforward task. While the native pronunciation of the name is the favored one, the origin of the name is not always clear, nor the definition of the pronunciation. Additionally, the mapping of the native pronunciation to the phoneme set used by the Finnish ASR system can only be an approximation, as well as the pronunciations that the Finnish speakers are able to produce. In future work we will study new methods to model the pronunciation of the foreign names and perform evaluations also in speech retrieval where the recognition of names have particular importance.

References

B. Ahmed. 2005. *Detection of Foreign Words and Names in Written Text.* Doctoral thesis, Pace University.

M. Bisani and H. Ney. 2008. *Joint-Sequence Models for Grapheme-to-Phoneme Conversion.* Speech Communication, vol. 50, Issue 5, pp. 434-451.

M. Creutz and K. Lagus. 2005. *Unsupervised Morpheme Segmentation and Morphology Induction from Text Corpora using Morfessor 1.0.* Technical Report A81, Publications in Computer and Information Science, Helsinki University of Technology.

T. Hirsimäki, J. Pylkkönen, and M. Kurimo 2009. *Importance of High-order N-gram Models in Morph-based Speech Recognition.* IEEE Trans. Audio, Speech and Lang., pp. 724-732, vol. 17.

V. Siivola, T. Hirsimäki and S. Virpioja. 2007. *On Growing and Pruning Kneser-Ney Smoothed N-Gram Models.* IEEE Trans. Audio, Speech and Lang., Vol. 15, No. 5.

Large-scale discriminative language model reranking for voice-search

Preethi Jyothi
The Ohio State University
Columbus, OH
jyothi@cse.ohio-state.edu

Leif Johnson
UT Austin
Austin, TX
leif@cs.utexas.edu

Ciprian Chelba and **Brian Strope**
Google
Mountain View, CA
{ciprianchelba,bps}@google.com

Abstract

We present a distributed framework for large-scale discriminative language models that can be integrated within a large vocabulary continuous speech recognition (LVCSR) system using lattice rescoring. We intentionally use a weakened acoustic model in a baseline LVCSR system to generate candidate hypotheses for voice-search data; this allows us to utilize large amounts of unsupervised data to train our models. We propose an efficient and scalable MapReduce framework that uses a perceptron-style distributed training strategy to handle these large amounts of data. We report small but significant improvements in recognition accuracies on a standard voice-search data set using our discriminative reranking model. We also provide an analysis of the various parameters of our models including model size, types of features, size of partitions in the MapReduce framework with the help of supporting experiments.

1 Introduction

The language model is a critical component of an automatic speech recognition (ASR) system that assigns probabilities or scores to word sequences. It is typically derived from a large corpus of text via maximum likelihood estimation in conjunction with some smoothing constraints. N-gram models have become the most dominant form of LMs in most ASR systems. Although these models are robust, scalable and easy to build, we illustrate a limitation with the following example from voice-search. We expect a low probability for an ungrammatical or implausible word sequence. However, for a trigram like "a navigate to", a backoff trigram LM gives a fairly large LM log probability of -0.266 because both "a" and "navigate to" are popular words in voice-search! Discriminative language models (DLMs) attempt to directly optimize error rate by rewarding features that appear in low error hypotheses and penalizing features in misrecognized hypotheses. The trigram "a navigate to" receives a fairly large negative weight of -6.5 thus decreasing its chances of appearing as an ASR output. There have been numerous approaches towards estimating DLMs for large vocabulary continuous speech recognition (LVCSR) (Roark et al., 2004; Gao et al., 2005; Zhou et al., 2006).

There are two central issues that we discuss regarding DLMs. Firstly, DLM training requires large amounts of parallel data (in the form of correct transcripts and candidate hypotheses output by an ASR system) to be able to effectively compete with n-gram LMs trained on large amounts of text. This data could be simulated using voice-search logs that are confidence-filtered from a baseline ASR system to obtain reference transcripts. However, this data is perfectly discriminated by first pass features and leaves little room for learning. We propose a novel training strategy of using lattices generated with a weaker acoustic model (henceforth referred to as *weakAM*) than the one used to generate reference transcripts for the unsupervised parallel data (referred to as the *strongAM*). This provides us with enough errors to derive large numbers of potentially useful word features; this is akin to using a weak LM in discriminative acoustic modeling to give more room for diversity in the word lattices resulting in better generalization (Schlüter et al., 1999). We conduct experiments to verify whether these *weakAM*-trained models will provide performance gains on rescoring lattices from a standard test set generated using *strongAM* (discussed in Section 3.3).

The second issue is that discriminative estimation of LMs is computationally more intensive than regular N-gram LM estimation. The advent of distributed learning algorithms (Mann et al., 2009; McDonald et al., 2010; Hall et al., 2010) and supporting parallel computing infrastructure like MapReduce (Ghemawat and Dean, 2004) has made it increasingly feasible to use large amounts of parallel data to train DLMs. We implement a distributed training strategy for the perceptron algorithm (introduced by McDonald et al. (2010) using the MapReduce framework. Our design choices for the MapReduce implementation are specified in Section 2.2 along with its modular nature thus enabling us to experiment with different variants of the distributed structured perceptron algorithm. Some of the descriptions in this paper have been adapted from previous work (Jyothi et al., 2012).

2 The distributed DLM framework: Training and Implementation details

2.1 Learning algorithm

We aim to allow the estimation of large scale distributed models, similar in size to the ones in Brants et al. (2007). To this end, we make use of a distributed training strategy for the structured perceptron to train our DLMs (McDonald et al., 2010). Our model consists of a high-dimensional feature vector function $\mathbf{\Phi}$ that maps an (utterance, hypothesis) pair (x, y) to a vector in $\mathbb{R}^d$, and a vector of model parameters, $\mathbf{w} \in \mathbb{R}^d$. Our goal is to find model parameters such that given x, and a set of candidate hypotheses $\mathcal{Y}$ (typically, as a word lattice or an N-best list that is obtained from a first pass recognizer), $\text{argmax}_{y \in \mathcal{Y}} \mathbf{w} \cdot \mathbf{\Phi}(x, y)$ would be the $y \in \mathcal{Y}$ that minimizes the error rate between y and the correct hypothesis for x. For our experiments, the feature vector $\mathbf{\Phi}(x, y)$ consists of AM and LM costs for y from the lattice $\mathcal{Y}$ for x), as well as "word features" which count the number of times different N-grams (of order up to 5 in our experiments) occur in y.

In principle, such a model can be trained using the conventional structured perceptron algorithm (Collins, 2002). This is an online learning algorithm which continually updates $\mathbf{w}$ as it processes the training instances one at a time, over multiple training epochs. Given a training utterance $\{x_i, y_i\}$ ($y_i \in \mathcal{Y}_i$ has the lowest error rate with respect to the reference transcription for x_i, among all hypotheses in the lattice $\mathcal{Y}_i$ for x_i), if $\tilde{y}_i^* := \text{argmax}_{y \in \mathcal{Y}_i} \mathbf{w} \cdot \mathbf{\Phi}(x_i, y)$ is not y_i, $\mathbf{w}$ is updated to increase the weights corresponding to features in y_i and decrease the weights of features in $\tilde{y}_i^*$. During evaluation, we use parameters averaged over all utterances and over all training epochs. This was shown to give substantial improvements in previous work (Collins, 2002; Roark et al., 2004).

Unfortunately, the conventional perceptron algorithm takes impractically long for the amount of training examples we have. We make use of a distributed training strategy for the structured perceptron that was first introduced in McDonald et al. (2010). The iterative parameter mixing strategy used in this paradigm can be explained as follows: the training data $\mathcal{T} = \{x_i, y_i\}_{i=1}^{\mathcal{N}}$ is suitably partitioned into $\mathcal{C}$ disjoint sets $\mathcal{T}_1, \ldots, \mathcal{T}_\mathcal{C}$. Then, a structured perceptron model is trained on each data set in parallel. After one training epoch, the parameters in the $\mathcal{C}$ sets are mixed together (using a "mixture coefficient" μ_i for each set $\mathcal{T}_i$) and returned to each perceptron model for the next training epoch where the parameter vector is initialized with these new mixed weights. This is formally described in Algorithm 1; we call it "*Distributed Perceptron*". We also experiment with two other variants of distributed perceptron training, "*Naive Distributed Perceptron*" and "*Averaged Distributed Perceptron*". These models easily lend themselves to be implemented using the distributed infrastructure provided by the MapReduce framework. The following section describes this infrastructure in greater detail.

2.2 MapReduce implementation details

We propose a distributed infrastructure using MapReduce (Ghemawat and Dean, 2004) to train our large-scale DLMs on terabytes of data. The MapReduce (Ghemawat and Dean, 2004) paradigm, adapted from a specialized functional programming construct, is specialized for use over clusters with

Algorithm 1 Distributed Perceptron (McDonald et al., 2010)

Require: Training samples $\mathcal{T} = \{x_i, y_i\}_{i=1}^{\mathcal{N}}$

$\mathbf{w}^0 := [0, \ldots, 0]$
Partition $\mathcal{T}$ into $\mathcal{C}$ parts, $\mathcal{T}_1, \ldots, \mathcal{T}_\mathcal{C}$
$[\mu_1, \ldots, \mu_\mathcal{C}] := [\frac{1}{\mathcal{C}}, \ldots, \frac{1}{\mathcal{C}}]$
for $t := 1$ to T **do**
    for $c := 1$ to $\mathcal{C}$ **do**
        $\mathbf{w} := \mathbf{w}^{t-1}$
        for $j := 1$ to $|\mathcal{T}_c|$ **do**
            $\tilde{y}_{c,j}^t := \text{argmax}_y\, \mathbf{w} \cdot \mathbf{\Phi}(x_{c,j}, y)$
            $\boldsymbol{\delta} := \mathbf{\Phi}(x_{c,j}, y_{c,j}) - \mathbf{\Phi}(x_{c,j}, \tilde{y}_{c,j}^t)$
            $\mathbf{w} := \mathbf{w} + \boldsymbol{\delta}$
        end for
        $\mathbf{w}_c^t := \mathbf{w}$
    end for
    $\mathbf{w}^t := \sum_{c=1}^{\mathcal{C}} \mu_c \mathbf{w}_c^t$
end for
return $\mathbf{w}^T$

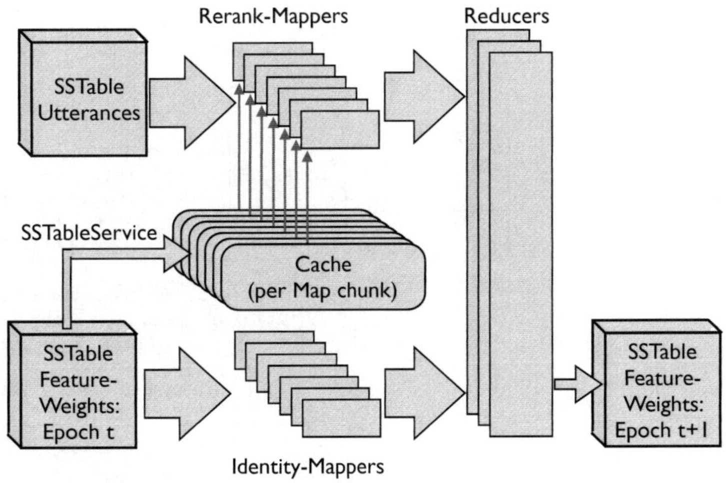

Figure 1: MapReduce implementation of reranking using discriminative language models.

a large number of nodes. Chu et al. (2007) have demonstrated that many standard machine learning algorithms can be phrased as MapReduce tasks, thus illuminating the versatility of this framework. In relation to language models, Brants et al. (2007) recently proposed a distributed MapReduce infrastructure to build Ngram language models having up to 300 billion n-grams. We take inspiration from this evidence of being able to build very large models and use the MapReduce infrastructure for our DLMs. Also, the MapReduce paradigm allows us to easily fit different variants of our learning algorithm in a modular fashion by only making small changes to the MapReduce functions.

In the MapReduce framework, any computation is expressed as two user-defined functions: *Map* and *Reduce*. The *Map* function takes as input a key/value pair and processes it using user-defined functions to generate a set of intermediate key/value pairs. The *Reduce* function receives all intermediate pairs that are associated with the same key value. The distributed nature of this framework comes from the ability to invoke the *Map* function on different parts of the input data simultaneously. Since the framework assures that all the values corresponding to a given key will be accummulated at the end of all the *Map* invocations on the input data, different machines can simultaneously execute the *Reduce* to operate on different parts of the intermediate data.

Any MapReduce application typically implements *Mapper/Reducer* interfaces to provide the desired *Map/Reduce* functionalities. For our models, we use two different Mappers (as illustrated in Figure 1) to compute feature weights for one training epoch. The *Rerank-Mapper* receives as input a set of training utterances and also requests for feature weights computed in the previous training epoch. *Rerank-Mapper* then computes feature updates for the given training data (the subset of the training data received by a single *Rerank-Mapper* instance will be henceforth referred to as a "Map chunk"). We also have a second *Identity-Mapper* that receives feature weights from the previous training epoch and directly maps the inputs to outputs which are provided to the *Reducer*. The *Reducer* combines the outputs from both *Rerank-Mapper* and *Identity-Mapper* and outputs the feature weights for the current training epoch. These output feature weights are persisted on disk in the form of SSTables that are an efficient abstraction to store large numbers of key-value pairs.

The features corresponding to a Map chunk at the end of training epoch need to be made available to *Rerank-Mapper* in the subsequent training epoch. Instead of accessing the features on demand from the SSTables that store these feature weights, every *Rerank-Mapper* stores the features needed for the current Map chunk in a cache. Though the number

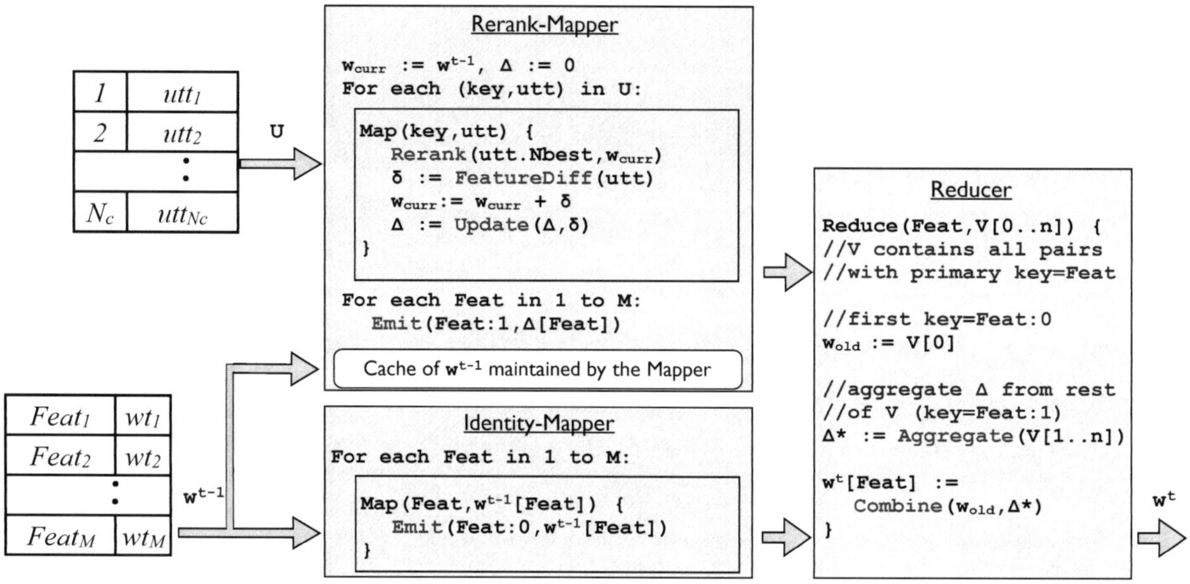

Figure 2: Details of the Mapper and Reducer.

Naive Distributed Perceptron:

- Update(Δ, δ) returns $\Delta + \delta$.
- Aggregate$([\Delta_1^t, \ldots, \Delta_C^t])$ returns $\Delta^* = \sum_{c=1}^{C} \Delta_c^t$.
- Combine(w_{NP}^{t-1}, Δ^*) returns $w_{NP}^{t-1} + \Delta^*$.

Distributed Perceptron:

- Update and Combine are as for the *Naive Distributed Perceptron*.
- Aggregate$([\Delta_1^t, \ldots, \Delta_C^t])$ returns $\Delta^* = \sum_{c=1}^{C} \mu_c \Delta_c^t$.

Averaged Distributed Perceptron: Here, $w^t = (w_{AV}^t, w_{DP}^t)$, and $\Delta = (\boldsymbol{\beta}, \boldsymbol{\alpha})$ contain pairs of values; $\boldsymbol{\alpha}$ is used to maintain w_{DP}^t and $\boldsymbol{\beta}$, both of which in turn are used to maintain w_{AV}^t ($\boldsymbol{\alpha}_c^t$ plays the role of Δ_c^t in *Distributed Perceptron*). Only w_{AV}^t is used in the final evaluation and only w_{DP}^t is used during training.

- Update$((\boldsymbol{\beta}, \boldsymbol{\alpha}), \delta)$ returns $(\boldsymbol{\beta} + \boldsymbol{\alpha} + \delta, \boldsymbol{\alpha} + \delta)$.
- Aggregate$([\Delta_1^t, \ldots, \Delta_C^t])$ where $\Delta_c^t = (\boldsymbol{\beta}_c^t, \boldsymbol{\alpha}_c^t)$, returns $\Delta^* = (\boldsymbol{\beta}^*, \boldsymbol{\alpha}^*)$ where $\boldsymbol{\beta}^* = \sum_{c=1}^{C} \boldsymbol{\beta}_c^t$, and $\boldsymbol{\alpha}^* = \sum_{c=1}^{C} \mu_c \boldsymbol{\alpha}_c^t$.
- Combine$((w_{AV}^{t-1}, w_{DP}^{t-1}), (\boldsymbol{\beta}^*, \boldsymbol{\alpha}^*))$ returns $(\frac{t-1}{t} w_{AV}^{t-1} + \frac{1}{t} w_{DP}^{t-1} + \frac{1}{Nt}\boldsymbol{\beta}^*, w_{DP}^{t-1} + \boldsymbol{\alpha}^*)$.

Figure 3: Update, Aggregate and Combine procedures for the three variants of the Distributed Perceptron algorithm.

of features stored in the SSTables are determined by the total number of training utterances, the number of features that are accessed by a *Rerank-Mapper* instance are only proportional to the chunk size and can be cached locally. This is an important implementation choice because it allows us to estimate very large distributed models: the bottleneck is no longer the total model size but rather the cache size that is in turn controlled by the Map chunk size. Section 3.2 discusses in more detail about different model sizes and the effects of varying Map chunk size on recognition performance.

Figure 1 is a schematic diagram of our entire framework; Figure 2 shows a more detailed representation of a single *Rerank-Mapper*, an *Identity-Mapper* and a *Reducer*, with the pseudocode of these interfaces shown inside their respective boxes. *Identity-Mapper* gets feature weights from the previous training epoch as input ($\mathbf{w}^t$) and passes them to the output unchanged. *Rerank-Mapper* calls the function Rerank that takes an N-best list of a training utterance (**utt.Nbest**) and the current feature weights

($\mathbf{w}_{curr}$) as input and reranks the N-best list to obtain the best scoring hypothesis. If this differs from the correct transcript for utt, FeatureDiff computes the difference in feature vectors corresponding to the two hypotheses (we call it δ) and $\mathbf{w}_{curr}$ is incremented with δ. Emit is the output function of a Mapper that outputs a processed key/value pair. For every feature Feat, both *Identity-Mapper* and *Rerank-Mapper* also output a secondary key (0 or 1, respectively); this is denoted as Feat:0 and Feat:1. At the *Reducer*, its inputs arrive sorted according to the secondary key; thus, the feature weight corresponding to Feat from the previous training epoch produced by *Identity-Mapper* will necessarily arrive before Feat's current updates from the *Rerank-Mapper*. This ensures that $\mathbf{w}^{t+1}$ is updated correctly starting with $\mathbf{w}^t$. The functions Update, Aggregate and Combine are explained in the context of three variants of the distributed perceptron algorithm in Figure 3.

2.2.1 MapReduce variants of the distributed perceptron algorithm

Our MapReduce setup described in the previous section allows for different variants of the distributed perceptron training algorithm to be implemented easily. We experimented with three slightly differing variants of a distributed training strategy for the structured perceptron, *Naive Distributed Perceptron*, *Distributed Perceptron* and *Averaged Distributed Perceptron*; these are defined in terms of Update, Aggregate and Combine in Figure 3 where each variant can be implemented by plugging in these definitions from Figure 3 into the pseudocode shown in Figure 2. We briefly describe the functionalities of these three variants. The weights at the end of a training epoch t for a single feature f are $(w^t_{NP}, w^t_{DP}, w^t_{AV})$ corresponding to *Naive Distributed Perceptron*, *Distributed Perceptron* and *Averaged Distributed Perceptron*, respectively; $\phi(\cdot,\cdot)$ correspond to feature f's value in $\mathbf{\Phi}$ from Algorithm 1. Below, $\delta^t_{c,j} = \phi(x_{c,j}, y_{c,j}) - \phi(x_{c,j}, \tilde{y}^t_{c,j})$ and $\mathcal{N}_c$ = number of utterances in Map chunk $\mathcal{T}_c$.

Naive Distributed Perceptron: At the end of epoch t, the weight increments in that epoch from all map chunks are added together and added to w^{t-1}_{NP} to obtain w^t_{NP}.

Distributed Perceptron: Here, instead of adding increments from the map chunks, at the end of epoch t, they are averaged together using weights μ_c, $c = 1$ to $\mathcal{C}$, and used to increment w^{t-1}_{DP} to w^t_{DP}.

Averaged Distributed Perceptron: In this variant, firstly, all epochs are carried out as in the Distributed Perceptron algorithm above. But at the end of t epochs, all the weights encountered during the whole process, over all utterances and all chunks, are averaged together to obtain the final weight w^t_{AV}. Formally,

$$w^t_{AV} = \frac{1}{\mathcal{N}\cdot t}\sum_{t'=1}^{t}\sum_{c=1}^{\mathcal{C}}\sum_{j=1}^{\mathcal{N}_c} w^{t'}_{c,j},$$

where $w^t_{c,j}$ refers to the current weight for map chunk c, in the tth epoch after processing j utterances and $\mathcal{N}$ is the total number of utterances. In our implementation, we maintain only the weight w^{t-1}_{DP} from the previous epoch, the cumulative increment $\gamma^t_{c,j} = \sum_{k=1}^{j}\delta^t_{c,k}$ so far in the current epoch, and a running average w^{t-1}_{AV}. Note that, for all c, j, $w^t_{c,j} = w^{t-1}_{DP} + \gamma^t_{c,j}$, and hence

$$\begin{aligned}\mathcal{N}t\cdot w^t_{AV} &= \mathcal{N}(t-1)w^{t-1}_{AV} + \sum_{c=1}^{\mathcal{C}}\sum_{j=1}^{\mathcal{N}_c} w^t_{c,j}\\ &= \mathcal{N}(t-1)w^{t-1}_{AV} + \mathcal{N}w^{t-1}_{DP} + \sum_{c=1}^{\mathcal{C}}\boldsymbol{\beta}^t_c\end{aligned}$$

where $\boldsymbol{\beta}^t_c = \sum_{j=1}^{\mathcal{N}_c}\gamma^t_{c,j}$. Writing $\boldsymbol{\beta}^* = \sum_{c=1}^{\mathcal{C}}\boldsymbol{\beta}^t_c$, we have $w^t_{AV} = \frac{t-1}{t}w^{t-1}_{AV} + \frac{1}{t}w^{t-1}_{DP} + \frac{1}{\mathcal{N}t}\boldsymbol{\beta}^*$.

3 Experiments and Results

Our DLMs are evaluated in two ways: 1) we extract a development set (*weakAM-dev*) and a test set (*weakAM-test*) from the speech data that is re-decoded with a *weakAM* to evaluate our learning setup, and 2) we use a standard voice-search test set (*v-search-test*) (Strope et al., 2011) to evaluate actual ASR performance on voice-search. More details regarding our experimental setup along with a discussion of our experiments and results are described in the rest of the section.

3.1 Experimental setup

We generate training lattices using speech data that is re-decoded with a *weakAM* acoustic model and

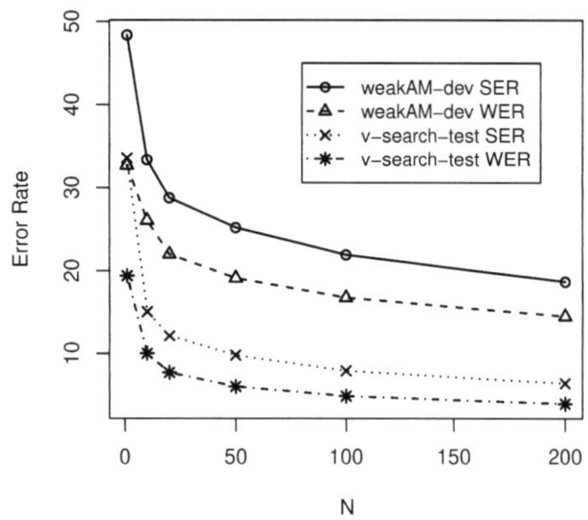

Figure 4: Oracle error rates at word/sentence level for *weakAM-dev* with the weak AM and *v-search-test* with the baseline AM.

a baseline language model. We use maximum likelihood trained single mixture Gaussians for our *weakAM*. And, we use a sufficiently small baseline LM ($\sim$21 million n-grams) to allow for subreal time lattice generation on the training data with a small memory footprint, without compromising on its strength. Chelba et al. (2010) demonstrate that it takes much larger LMs to get a significant relative gain in WER. Our largest models are trained on 87,000 hours of speech, or $\sim$350 million words (*weakAM-train*) obtained by filtering voice-search logs at 0.8 confidence, and re-decoding the speech data with a *weakAM* to generate N-best lists. We set aside a part of this *weakAM-train* data to create *weakAM-dev* and *weakAM-test*: these data sets consist of 328,460/316,992 utterances, or 1,182,756/1,129,065 words, respectively. We use a manually-transcribed, standard voice-search test set (*v-search-test* (Strope et al., 2011)) consisting of 27,273 utterances, or 87,360 words to evaluate actual ASR performance using our *weakAM*-trained models. All voice-search data used in the experiments is anonymized.

Figure 4 shows oracle error rates, both at the sentence and word level, using N-best lists of utterances in *weakAM-dev* and *v-search-test*. These error rates are obtained by choosing the best of the top N hypotheses that is either an exact match (for sentence error rate) or closest in edit distance (for word error rate) to the correct transcript. The N-best lists for *weakAM-dev* are generated using a weak AM and N-best lists for *v-search-test* are generated using the baseline (strong) AM. Figure 4 shows these error rates plotted against a varying threshold N for the N-best lists. Note there are sufficient word errors in the *weakAM* data to train DLMs; also, we observe that the plot flattens out after N=100, thus informing us that N=100 is a reasonable threshold to use when training our DLMs.

Experiments in Section 3.2 involve evaluating our learning setup using *weakAM-dev/test*. We then investigate whether improvements on *weakAM-dev/test* translate to *v-search-test* where N-best are generated using the *strongAM*, and scored against *manual* transcripts using fully fledged text normalization instead of the string edit distance used in training the DLM. More details about the implications of this text normalization on WER can be found in Section 3.3.

3.2 Evaluating our DLM rescoring framework on *weakAM-dev/test*

Improvements on *weakAM-dev* using different variants of training for the DLMs

We evaluate the performance of all the variants of the distributed perceptron algorithm described in Section 2.2 over ten training epochs using a DLM trained on $\sim$20,000 hours of speech with trigram word features. Figure 5 shows the drop in WER for all the three variants. We observe that the *Naive Distributed Perceptron* gives modest improvements in WER compared to the baseline WER of 32.5%. However, averaging over the number of Map chunks as in the *Distributed Perceptron* or over the total number of utterances and training epochs as in the *Averaged Distributed Perceptron* significantly improves recognition performance; this is in line with the findings reported in Collins (2002) and McDonald et al. (2010) of averaging being an effective way of adding regularization to the perceptron algorithm.

Our best-performing *Distributed Perceptron* model gives a 4.7% absolute ($\sim$15% relative) improvement over the baseline WER of 1-best hypotheses in *weakAM-dev*. This, however, could be attributed to a combination of factors: the use of large amounts of additional training data for the DLMs or the discriminative nature of the model. In order to isolate the improvements brought upon mainly by the second factor, we build an ML trained backoff trigram LM (ML-3gram) using the

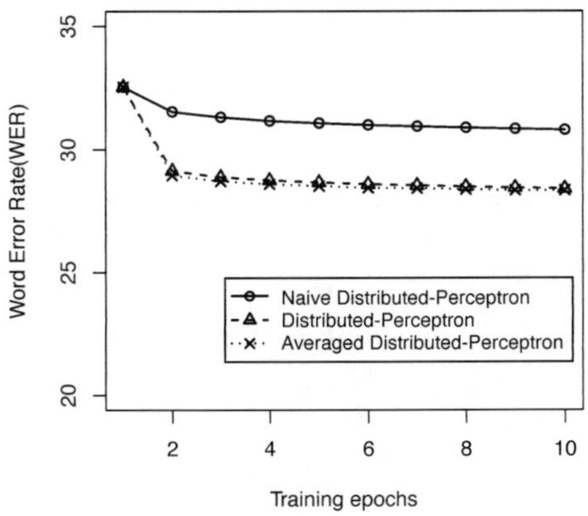

Figure 5: Word error rates on *weakAM-dev* using *Perceptron*, *Distributed Perceptron* and *AveragedPerceptron* models.

reference transcripts of all the utterances used to train the DLMs. The N-best lists in *weakAM-dev* are reranked using ML-3gram probabilities linearly interpolated with the LM probabilities from the lattices. We also experiment with a log-linear interpolation of the models; this performs slightly worse than rescoring with linear interpolation.

Table 1: WERs on *weakAM-dev* using the baseline 1-best system, ML-3gram and DLM-1/2/3gram.

Data set	Baseline (%)	ML-3gram (%)	DLM-1gram (%)	DLM-2gram (%)	DLM-3gram (%)
weakAM-dev	32.5	29.8	29.5	28.3	27.8

Impact of varying orders of N-gram features

Table 1 shows that our best performing model (DLM-3gram) gives a significant $\sim$2% absolute ($\sim$6% relative) improvement over ML-3gram. We also observe that most of the improvements come from the unigram and bigram features. We do not expect higher order N-gram features to significantly help recognition performance; we further confirm this by building DLM-4gram and DLM-5gram that use up to 4-gram and 5-gram word features, respectively. Table 2 gives the progression of WERs for six epochs using DLM-3gram, DLM-4gram and DLM-5gram showing minute improvements as we increase the order of Ngram features from 3 to 5.

Table 2: WERs on *weakAM-dev* using DLM-3gram, DLM-4gram and DLM-5gram of six training epochs.

Iteration	DLM-3gram (%)	DLM-4gram (%)	DLM-5gram (%)
1	32.53	32.53	32.53
2	29.52	29.47	29.46
3	29.26	29.23	29.22
4	29.11	29.08	29.06
5	29.01	28.98	28.96
6	28.95	28.90	28.87

Impact of model size on WER

We experiment with varying amounts of training data to build our DLMs and assess the impact of model size on WER. Table 3 shows each model along with its size (measured in total number of word features), coverage on *weakAM-test* in percent of tokens (number of word features in *weakAM-test* that are in the model) and WER on *weakAM-test*. As expected, coverage increases with increasing model size with a corresponding tiny drop in WER as the model size increases. To give an estimate of the time complexity of our MapReduce, we note that Model1 was trained in $\approx$1 hour on 200 mappers with a Map chunk size of 2GB. "Larger models", built by increasing the number of training utterances used to train the DLMs, do not yield significant gains in accuracy. We need to find a good way of adjusting the model capacity with increasing amounts of data.

Impact of varying Map chunk sizes

We also experiment with varying Map chunk sizes to determine its effect on WER. Figure 6 shows WERs on *weakAM-dev* using our best *Distributed Perceptron* model with different Map chunk sizes (64MB, 512MB, 2GB). For clarity, we examine two limit cases: a) using a single Map chunk for the entire training data is equivalent to the conventional structured perceptron and b) using a single training in-

Table 3: WERs on *weakAM-test* using DLMs of varying sizes.

Model	Size (in millions)	Coverage (%)	WER (%)
Baseline	21M	-	39.08
Model1	65M	74.8	34.18
Model2	135M	76.9	33.83
Model3	194M	77.8	33.74
Model4	253M	78.4	33.68

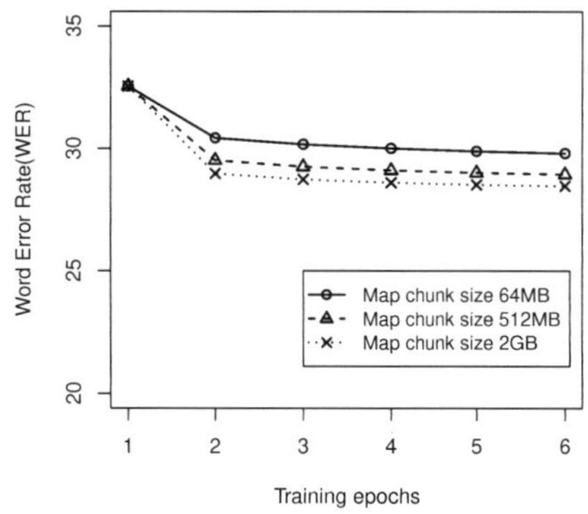

Figure 6: Word error rates on *weakAM-dev* using varying Map chunk sizes of 64MB, 512MB and 2GB.

stance per Map chunk is equivalent to batch training. We observe that moving from 64MB to 512MB significantly improves WER and the rate of improvement in WER decreases when we increase the Map chunk size further to 2GB. We attribute these reductions in WER with increasing Map chunk size to on-line parameter updates being done on increasing amounts of training samples in each Map chunk.

3.3 Evaluating ASR performance on *v-search-test* using DLM rescoring

We evaluate our best *Distributed Perceptron* DLM model on *v-search-test* lattices that are generated using a strong AM. We hope that the large relative gains on *weakAM-dev/test* translate to similar gains on this standard voice-search data set as well. Table 4 shows the WERs on both *weakAM-test* and *v-search-test* using Model 1 (from Table 3)[1]. We observe a small but statistically significant ($p < 0.05$) reduction (~2% relative) in WER on *v-search-test* over reranking with a linearly interpolated ML-3gram. This is encouraging because we attain this improvement using training lattices that were generated using a considerably weaker AM.

Table 4: WERs on *weakAM-test* and *v-search-test*.

Data set	Baseline (%)	ML-3gram (%)	DLM-3gram (%)
weakAM-test	39.1	36.7	34.2
v-search-test	14.9	14.6	14.3

It is instructive to analyze why the relative gains in performance on *weakAM-dev/test* do not translate to *v-search-test*. Our DLMs are built using N-best outputs from the recognizer that live in the "spoken domain" (SD) and the manually transcribed *v-search-data* transcripts live in the "written domain" (WD). The normalization of training data from WD to SD is as described in Chelba et al. (2010); inverse text normalization (ITN) undoes most of that when moving text from SD to WD, and it is done in a heuristic way. There is ~2% absolute reduction in WER when we move the N-best from SD to WD via ITN; this is how WER on *v-search-test* is computed by the voice-search evaluation code. Contrary to this, in DLM training we compute WERs using string edit distance between test data transcripts and the N-best hypotheses and thus we ignore the mismatch between domains WD and SD. It is quite likely that part of what the DLM learns is to pick N-best hypotheses that come closer to WD, but may not truly result in WER gains after ITN. This would explain part of the mismatch between the large relative gains on *weakAM-dev/test* compared to the smaller gains on *v-search-test*. We could correct for this by applying ITN to the N-best lists from SD to move to WD before computing the oracle best in the list. An even more desirable solution is to build the LM directly on WD text; text normalization would be employed for pronunciation generation, but ITN is not needed anymore (the LM picks the most likely WD word string for homophone queries at recognition).

4 Conclusions

In this paper, we successfully build large-scale discriminative N-gram language models with lattices regenerated using a weak AM and derive small but significant gains in recognition performance on a voice-search task where the lattices are generated using a stronger AM. We use a very simple weak AM and this suggests that there is room for improvement if we use a slightly better "weak AM". Also, we have a scalable and efficient MapReduce implementation that is amenable to adapting minor changes to the training algorithm easily and allows for us to train large LMs. The latter functionality will be particularly useful if we generate the contrastive set by sampling from text instead of redecoding logs (Jyothi and Fosler-Lussier, 2010).

[1]We also experimented with the larger Model 4 and saw similar improvements on *v-search-test* as with Model 1.

References

Thorsten Brants, Ashok C. Popat, Peng Xu, Franz J. Och, and Jeffrey Dean. 2007. Large language models in machine translation. In *Proc. of EMNLP*, pages 858–867.

C. Chelba, J. Schalkwyk, T. Brants, V. Ha, B. Harb, W. Neveitt, C. Parada, and P. Xu. 2010. Query language modeling for voice search. In *Proc. of SLT*.

C.T. Chu, S.K. Kim, Y.A. Lin, Y.Y. Yu, G. Bradski, A.Y. Ng, and K. Olukotun. 2007. Map-reduce for machine learning on multicore. *Proc. NIPS*, 19:281.

M. Collins. 2002. Discriminative training methods for hidden markov models: Theory and experiments with perceptron algorithms. In *Proc. EMNLP*.

J. Gao, H. Yu, W. Yuan, and P. Xu. 2005. Minimum sample risk methods for language modeling. In *Proc. of EMNLP*.

S. Ghemawat and J. Dean. 2004. Mapreduce: Simplified data processing on large clusters. In *Proc. OSDI*.

K.B. Hall, S. Gilpin, and G. Mann. 2010. MapReduce/Bigtable for distributed optimization. In *NIPS LCCC Workshop*.

P. Jyothi and E. Fosler-Lussier. 2010. Discriminative language modeling using simulated ASR errors. In *Proc. of Interspeech*.

P. Jyothi, L. Johnson, C. Chelba, and B. Strope. 2012. Distributed discriminative language models for Google voice-search. In *Proc. of ICASSP*.

G. Mann, R. McDonald, M. Mohri, N. Silberman, and D. Walker. 2009. Efficient large-scale distributed training of conditional maximum entropy models. *Proc. NIPS*.

R. McDonald, K. Hall, and G. Mann. 2010. Distributed training strategies for the structured perceptron. In *Proc. NAACL*.

B. Roark, M. Saraçlar, M. Collins, and M. Johnson. 2004. Discriminative language modeling with conditional random fields and the perceptron algorithm. In *Proc. ACL*.

R. Schlüter, B. Müller, F. Wessel, and H. Ney. 1999. Interdependence of language models and discriminative training. In *Proc. ASRU*.

B. Strope, D. Beeferman, A. Gruenstein, and X. Lei. 2011. Unsupervised testing strategies for ASR. In *Proc. of Interspeech*.

Z. Zhou, J. Gao, F.K. Soong, and H. Meng. 2006. A comparative study of discriminative methods for reranking LVCSR N-best hypotheses in domain adaptation and generalization. In *Proc. ICASSP*.

Revisiting the Case for Explicit Syntactic Information in Language Models

Ariya Rastrow, Sanjeev Khudanpur, Mark Dredze
Human Language Technology Center of Excellence,
Center for Language and Speech Processing, Johns Hopkins University
Baltimore, MD USA
{ariya,khudanpur,mdredze}@jhu.edu

Abstract

Statistical language models used in deployed systems for speech recognition, machine translation and other human language technologies are almost exclusively n-gram models. They are regarded as *linguistically naïve*, but estimating them from any amount of text, large or small, is straightforward. Furthermore, they have doggedly matched or outperformed numerous competing proposals for *syntactically well-motivated* models. This unusual resilience of n-grams, as well as their weaknesses, are examined here. It is demonstrated that n-grams are good word-predictors, even linguistically speaking, in a large majority of word-positions, and it is suggested that to improve over n-grams, one must explore syntax-aware (or other) language models that focus on positions where n-grams are weak.

1 Introduction

Language models (LM) are crucial components in tasks that require the generation of coherent natural language text, such as automatic speech recognition (ASR) and machine translation (MT). Most language models rely on simple n-gram statistics and a wide range of smoothing and backoff techniques (Chen and Goodman, 1998). State-of-the-art ASR systems use $(n-1)$-gram equivalence classification for the language model (which result in an n-gram language model).

While simple and efficient, it is widely believed that limiting the context to only the $(n-1)$ most recent words ignores the structure of language, and several statistical frameworks have been proposed to incorporate the "syntactic structure of language back into language modeling." Yet despite considerable effort on including longer-dependency features, such as syntax (Chelba and Jelinek, 2000; Khudanpur and Wu, 2000; Collins et al., 2005; Emami and Jelinek, 2005; Kuo et al., 2009; Filimonov and Harper, 2009), n-gram language models remain the dominant technique in automatic speech recognition and machine translation (MT) systems.

While intuition suggests syntax is important, the continued dominance of n-gram models could indicate otherwise. While no one would dispute that syntax informs word choice, perhaps sufficient information aggregated across a large corpus is available in the local context for n-gram models to perform well even without syntax. To clearly demonstrate the utility of syntactic information and the deficiency of n-gram models, we empirically show that n-gram LMs lose significant predictive power in positions where the syntactic relation spans beyond the n-gram context. This clearly shows a performance gap in n-gram LMs that could be bridged by syntax.

As a candidate syntactic LM we consider the Structured Language Model (SLM) (Chelba and Jelinek, 2000), one of the first successful attempts to build a statistical language model based on syntactic information. The SLM assigns a joint probability $P(W,T)$ to every word sequence W and every possible binary parse tree T, where T's terminals are words W with part-of-speech (POS) tags, and its internal nodes comprise non-terminal labels and lexical "heads" of phrases. Other approaches include using the exposed headwords in a maximum-entropy based LM (Khudanpur and Wu, 2000), using exposed headwords from full-sentence parse tree in a neural network based LM (Kuo et al., 2009), and the use of syntactic features in discriminative training (Rastrow et al., 2011). We show that the long-dependencies modeled by SLM, significantly improves the predictive power of the LM, specially in positions where the syntactic relation is beyond the reach of regular n-gram models.

2 Weaknesses of n-gram LMs

Consider the following sentence, which demonstrates why the $(n-1)$-gram equivalence classification of history in n-gram language models may be insufficient:

`<s> i asked the vice president for his endorsement </s>`

In an n-gram LM, the word `for` would be modeled based on a 3-gram or 4-gram history, such as `<vice president>` or `<the vice president>`. Given the *syntactic* relation between the preposition `for` and the verb `asked` (which together make a compound verb), the strongest evidence in the history (and hence the best classification of the history) for word `for` should be `<asked president>`, which is beyond the 4-gram LM. Clearly, the *syntactic relation* between a word position and the corresponding words in the history spans beyond the limited $(n-1)$-gram equivalence classification of the history.

This is but one of many examples used for motivating *syntactic features* (Chelba and Jelinek, 2000; Kuo et al., 2009) in language modeling. However, it is legitimate to ask if this deficiency could be overcome through sufficient data, that is, accurate statistics could somehow be gathered for the n-grams even without including syntactic information. We empirically show that $(n-1)$-gram equivalence classification of history is not adequate to predict these cases. Specifically, n-gram LMs lose predictive power in the positions where the *headword* relation, exposed by the syntactic structure, goes beyond $(n-1)$ previous words (in the history.)

We postulate the following three hypotheses:

Hypothesis 1 *There is a substantial difference in the predictive power of n-gram LMs at positions within a sentence where syntactic dependencies reach further back than the n-gram context versus positions where syntactic dependencies are local.*

Hypothesis 2 *This difference does not diminish by increasing training data by an order of magnitude.*

Hypothesis 3 *LMs that specifically target positions with syntactically distant dependencies will complement or improve over n-gram LMs for these positions.*

In the following section (Section 3), we present a set of experiments to support the hypotheses 1 and 2. Section 4 introduces a SLM which uses dependency structures followed by experiments in Section 5.

3 Experimental Evidence

In this section, we explain our experimental evidence for supporting the hypotheses stated above. First, Section 3.1 presents our experimental design where we use a statistical constituent parser to identify two types of word positions in a test data, namely positions where the headword syntactic relation spans beyond recent words in the history and positions where the headword syntactic relation is within the n-gram window. The performance of an n-gram LM is measured on both types of positions to show substantial difference in the predictive power of the LM in those positions. Section 3.3 describes the results and analysis of our experiments which supports our hypotheses.

Throughout the rest of the paper, we refer to a position where the headword syntactic relation reaches further back than the n-gram context as a *syntactically-distant* position and other type of positions is referred to as a *syntactically-local* position.

3.1 Design

Our experimental design is based on the idea of comparing the performance of n-gram LMs for *syntactically-distant* vs. *syntactically-local* . To this end, we first parse each sentence in the test set using a constituent parser, as illustrated by the example in Figure 1. For each word w_i in each sentence, we then check if the "syntactic heads" of the preceding constituents in the parse of $w_1, w_2, \cdots, w_{i-1}$ are within an $(n-1)$ window of w_i. In this manner, we split the test data into two disjoint sets, $\mathcal{M}$ and $\mathcal{N}$,

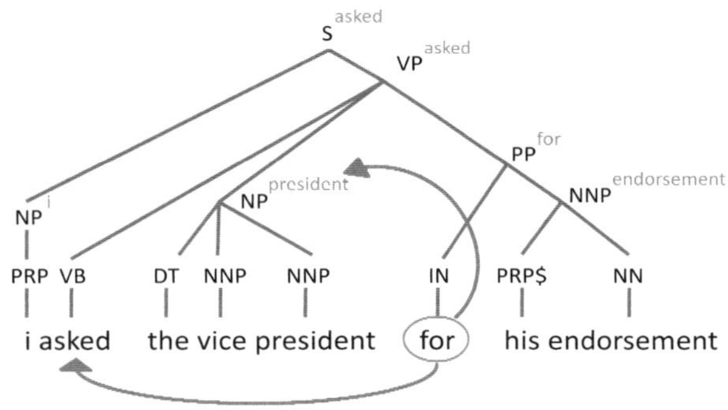

Figure 1: Example of a *syntactically distant* position in a sentence: the exposed headwords preceding `for` are $h.\text{w}_{-2}$ =`asked` and $h.\text{w}_{-1}$ = `president`, while the two preceding words are w_{i-2} = `vice` and w_{i-1} = `president`.

as follows,

$$\mathcal{M} = \{j|\text{positions s.t } h.\text{w}_{-1}, h.\text{w}_{-2} = w_{j-1}, w_{j-2}\}$$
$$\mathcal{N} = \{j|\text{positions s.t } h.\text{w}_{-1}, h.\text{w}_{-2} \neq w_{j-1}, w_{j-2}\}$$

Here, h_{-1} and h_{-2} correspond, respectively, to the two previous *exposed headwords* at position i, based on the syntactic structure. Therefore, $\mathcal{M}$ corresponds to the positions in the test data for which two previous *exposed heads* match exactly the two previous words. Whereas, $\mathcal{N}$ corresponds to the position where at least on of the *exposed heads* is further back in the history than the two previous words, possibly both.

To extract the exposed headwords at each position, we use a constituent parser to obtain the syntactic structure of a sentence followed by *headword percolation* procedure to get the headwords of corresponding syntactic phrases in the parse tree. The following method, described in (Kuo et al., 2009), is then used to extract exposed headwords from the history of position i from the full-sentence parse trees:

1. Start at the leaf corresponding to the word position (w_i) and the leaf corresponding to the previous context word (w_{i-1}).
2. From each leaf, go up the tree until the two paths meet at the lowest common ancestor (LCA).
3. Cut the link between the LCA and the child that is along the path from the context word w_{i-1}. The head word of the the LCA child, the one that is cut, is chosen as previous exposed headword $h.\text{w}_{-1}$.

These steps may be illustrated using the parse tree shown in Figure 1. Let us show the procedure for our example from Section 2. Figure 1 shows the corresponding parse tree of our example. Considering word position w_i=`for` and w_{i-1}=`president` and applying the above procedure, the LCA is the node $\text{VP}^{\textbf{asked}}$. Now, by cutting the link from $\text{VP}^{\textbf{asked}}$ to $\text{NP}^{\textbf{president}}$ the word `president` is obtained as the first exposed headword ($h.\text{w}_{-1}$).

After the first previous exposed headword has been extracted, the second exposed headword also can be obtained using the same procedure, with the constraint that the node corresponding the second headword is different from the first (Kuo et al., 2009). More precisely,

1. set $k = 2$
2. Apply the above headword extraction method between w_i and w_{i-k}.
3. if the extracted headword has previously been chosen, set $k = k + 1$ and go to step (2).
4. Otherwise, return the headword as $h.\text{w}_{-2}$.

Continuing with the example of Figure 1, after `president` is chosen as $h.\text{w}_{-1}$, `asked` is chosen as $h.\text{w}_{-2}$ of position `for` by applying the procedure above. Therefore, in this example the position corresponding to word `for` belongs to the set $\mathcal{N}$ as the two extracted exposed headwords (`asked,president`) are different from the two previous context words (`vice,president`).

After identifying sets $\mathcal{N}$ and $\mathcal{M}$ in our test data, we measure *perplexity* of n-gram LMs on $\mathcal{N}$, $\mathcal{M}$ and $\mathcal{N} \cup \mathcal{M}$ separately. That is,

$$\text{PPL}_{\mathcal{N}\cup\mathcal{M}} = \exp\left[-\frac{\sum_{i\in\mathcal{N}\cup\mathcal{M}} \log p(w_i|W_{i-n+1}^{i-1})}{|\mathcal{N}\cup\mathcal{M}|}\right]$$
$$\text{PPL}_{\mathcal{N}} = \exp\left[-\sum_{i\in\mathcal{N}} \frac{\log p(w_i|W_{i-n+1}^{i-1})}{|\mathcal{N}|}\right]$$
$$\text{PPL}_{\mathcal{M}} = \exp\left[-\sum_{i\in\mathcal{M}} \frac{\log p(w_i|W_{i-n+1}^{i-1})}{|\mathcal{M}|}\right],$$

where $p(w_i|w_{i-1}w_{i-2}\cdots w_{i-n+1})$ is the conditional probability calculated by an n-gram LM at position i and $|.|$ is the size (in number of words) of the corresponding portion of the test.

In addition, to show the performance of n-gram LMs as a function of training data size, we train different n-gram LMs on 10%,20%,$\cdots$,100% of a large corpus of text and report the PPL numbers using each trained LM with different training data size. For all sizes less than 100%, we select 10 random subset of the training corpus of the required size, and report the average perplexity of 10 n-gram models. This will enable us to observe the improvement of the n-gram LMs on as we increase the training data size. The idea is to test the hypothesis that not only is there significant gap between predictive power of the n-gram LMs on sets $\mathcal{N}$ and $\mathcal{M}$, but also that this difference does not diminish by adding more training data. In other words, we want to show that the problem is not due to lack of robust *estimation* of the model parameters but due to the fact that the included features in the model (n-grams) are not *informative* enough for the positions $\mathcal{N}$.

3.2 Setup

The n-gram LMs are built on $400M$ words from various Broadcast News (BN) data sources including (Chen et al., 2006): 1996 CSR Hub4 Language Model data, EARS BN03 closed captions, GALE Phase 2 Distillation GNG Evaluation Supplemental Multilingual data, Hub4 acoustic model training scripts (corresponding to the 300 Hrs), TDT4 closed captions, TDT4 newswire, GALE Broadcast Conversations, and GALE Broadcast News. All the LMs are trained using modified Kneser-Ney smoothing. To build the LMs, we sample from each source and build a source specific LM on the sampled data. The final LMs are then built by interpolating those LMs. Also, we do not apply any pruning to the trained LMs, a step that is often necessary for speech recognition but not so for perplexity measurement. The test set consists of the NIST rt04 evaluation data set, dev04f evaluation set, and rt03 evaluation set. The test data includes about $70K$ words.

We use the parser of (Huang and Harper, 2009), which achieves state-of-the-art performance on broadcast news data, to identify the word poisons that belong to $\mathcal{N}$ and $\mathcal{M}$, as was described in Section 3.1. The parser is trained on the Broadcast News treebank from Ontonotes (Weischedel et al., 2008) and the WSJ Penn Treebank (Marcus et al., 1993) along with self-training on 1996 Hub4 CSR (Garofolo et al., 1996) utterances.

3.3 Analysis

We found that $\frac{|\mathcal{N}|}{|\mathcal{N}\cup\mathcal{M}|} \approx 0.25$ in our test data. In other words, two previous exposed headwords go beyond 2-gram history for about 25% of the test data.

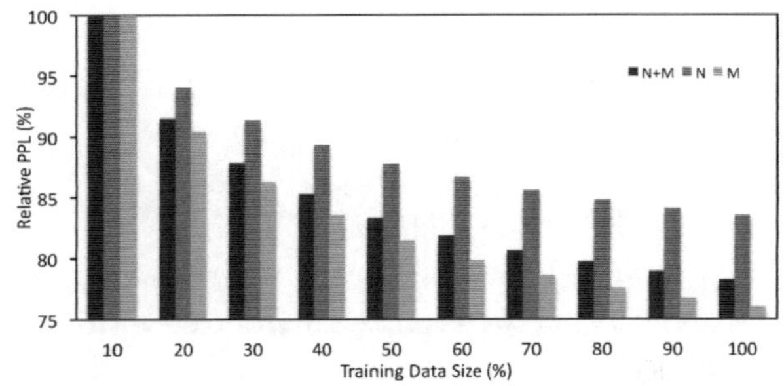

(a)

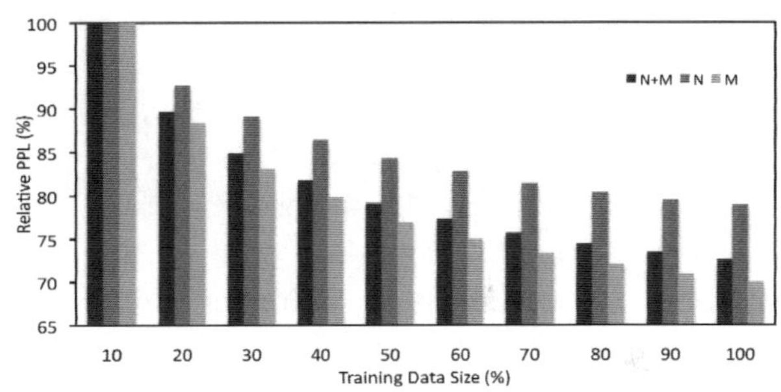

(b)

Figure 2: Reduction in perplexity with increasing training data size on the entire test set $\mathcal{N}+\mathcal{M}$, on its *syntactically local* subset $\mathcal{M}$, and the *syntactically distant* subset $\mathcal{N}$. The figure shows relative perplexity instead of absolute perplexity — 100% being the perplexity for the smallest training set size — so that (a) 3-gram and (b) 4-gram LMs may be directly compared.

We train 3-gram and 4-gram LMs on 10%,20%,$\cdots$,100% of the BN training data, where each 10% increase corresponds to about $40M$ words of training text data. Figure 2 shows reduction in perplexity with increasing training data size on the entire test set $\mathcal{N}+\mathcal{M}$, on its *syntactically local* subset $\mathcal{M}$, and the *syntactically distant* subset $\mathcal{N}$. The figure basically shows relative perplexity instead of absolute perplexity — 100% being the

Position in Test Set	Training Data Size			
	40M words		400M words	
	3-gram	4-gram	3-gram	4-gram
$\mathcal{M}$	166	153	126	107
$\mathcal{N}$	228	217	191	171
$\mathcal{N}+\mathcal{M}$	183	170	143	123
$\frac{PPL_{\mathcal{N}}}{PPL_{\mathcal{M}}}$	138%	142%	151%	161%

Table 1: Perplexity of 3-gram and 4-gram LMs on *syntactically local* ($\mathcal{M}$) and *syntactically distant* ($\mathcal{N}$) positions in the test set for different training data sizes, showing the sustained higher perplexity in distant v/s local positions.

perplexity for the smallest training set size — so the rate of improvement for 3-grams and 4-gram LMs can be compared. As can be seen from Figure 2, there is a substantial gap between the improvement rate of *perplexity* in syntactically distant positions compared to that in syntactically local positions (with 400M woods of training data, this gap is about 10% for both 3-gram and 4-gram LMs). In other words, increasing the training data size has much more effect on improving the predictive power of the model for the positions included in $\mathcal{M}$. Also, by comparing Figure 2(a) to 2(b) one can observe that the gap is not overcome by increasing the context length (using 4-gram features).

Also, to better illustrate the performance of the n-gram LMs for different portions of our test data, we report the absolute values of PPL results in Table 1. It can be seen that there exits a significant difference between *perplexity* of sets $\mathcal{N}$ and $\mathcal{M}$ and that the difference gets larger as we increase the training data size.

4 Dependency Language Models

To overcome the lack of predictive power of n-gram LMs in *syntactically-distant* positions, we use the SLM framework to build a long-span LM. Our hope is to show not only that long range syntactic dependencies improve over n-gram features, but also that the improvement is largely due to better predictive power in the syntactically distant positions $\mathcal{N}$.

Syntactic information may be encoded in terms of headwords and headtags of phrases, which may be extracted from a syntactic analysis of a sentence (Chelba and Jelinek, 2000; Kuo et al., 2009), such as a *dependency structure*. A dependency in a sentence holds between a *dependent* (or *modifier*) word and a *head* (or *governor*) word: the dependent *depends* on the head. These relations are encoded in a *dependency tree* (Figure 3), a directed graph where each edge (arc) encodes a head-dependent relation.

The specific parser used to obtain the syntactic structure is not important to our investigation. What is crucial, however, is that the parser proceeds left-to-right, and only hypothesized structures based on $w_1, \ldots, w_{i-1}$ are used by the SLM to predict w_i.

Similarly, the specific features used by the parser are also not important: more noteworthy is that the SLM uses $(h.\mathrm{w}_{-3}, h.\mathrm{w}_{-2}, h.\mathrm{w}_{-1})$ and their POS tags to predict w_i. The question is whether this yields lower perplexity than predicting w_i from $(w_{i-3}, w_{i-2}, w_{i-1})$.

For the sake of completeness, we next describe the parser and SLM in some detail, but either may be skipped without loss of continuity.

The Parser: We use the shift-reduce incremental dependency parser of (Sagae and Tsujii, 2007), which constructs a tree from a transition sequence governed by a maximum-entropy classifier. Shift-reduce parsing places input words into a queue Q and partially built structures are organized by a stack S. Shift and reduce actions consume the queue and build the output parse on the stack. The classifier g assigns probabilities to each action, and the probability of a state $p_g(\pi)$ can be computed as the product of the probabilities of a sequence of actions that resulted in the state. The parser therefore provides (multiple) syntactic analyses of the history $w_1, \ldots, w_{i-1}$ at each word position w_i.

The Dependency Language Model: Parser states at position w_i, called *history-states*, are denoted $\Pi_{-i} = \{\pi^0_{-i}, \pi^1_{-i} \cdots, \pi^{K_i}_{-i}\}$, where K_i is the total number of such states. Given Π_{-i}, the probability assignment for w_i is given by

$$p(w_i|W_{-i}) = \sum_{j=1}^{|\Pi_{-i}|} p\left(w_i|f(\pi^j_{-i})\right) p_g(\pi^j_{-i}|W_{-i}) \quad (1)$$

where, W_{-i} is the word history $w_1, \ldots, w_{i-1}$ for w_i, π^j_{-i} is the jth history-state of position i, $p_g(\pi^j_{-i}|W_{-i})$ is the probability assigned to π^j_{-i} by

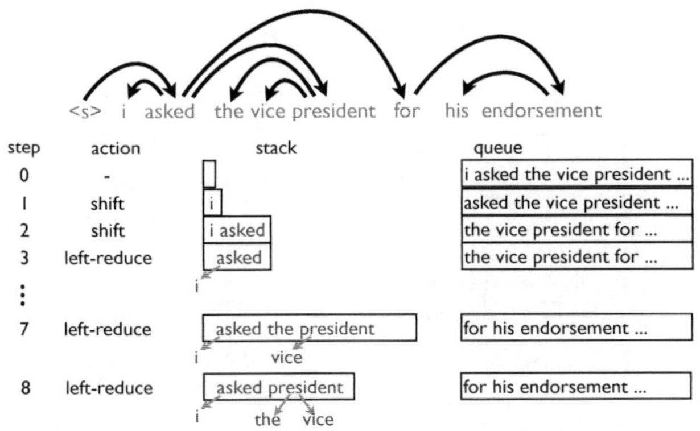

Figure 3: Actions of a shift-reduce parser to produce the dependency structure (up to the word `president`) shown above.

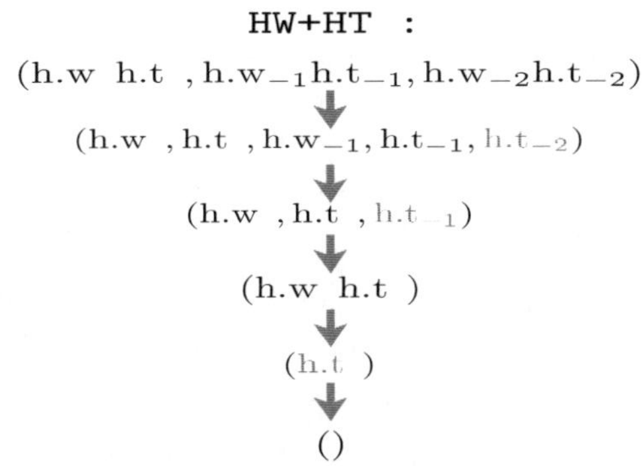

Figure 4: The hierarchal scheme of fine-to-coarse contexts used for Jelinek-Mercer smoothing in the SLM.

the parser, and $f(\pi^j_{-i})$ denotes an equivalence classification of the parser history-state, capturing features from π^j_{-i} that are useful for predicting w_i.

We restrict $f(\pi)$ to be based on only the heads of the partial trees $\{s_0\, s_1 \cdots\}$ in the stack. For example, in Figure 3, one possible parser state for predicting the word `for` is the entire stack shown after step 8, but we restrict $f(\cdot)$ to depend only on the headwords `asked/VB` and `president/NNP`.

Given a choice of $f(\cdot)$, the parameters of the model $p(w_i|f(\pi^j_{-i}))$ are estimated to maximize the log-likelihood of the training data $\mathcal{T}$ using the Baum-Welch algorithm (Baum, 1972), and the resulting estimate is denoted $p_{\mathrm{ML}}(w_i|f(\pi^j_{-i}))$.

The estimate $p_{\mathrm{ML}}(w|f(\cdot))$ must be smoothed to handle unseen events, which we do using the method of Jelinek and Mercer (1980). We use a fine-to-coarse hierarchy of features of the history-state as illustrated in Figure 4. With

$$f_M(\pi_{-i}) \;\rightarrow\; f_{M-1}(\pi_{-i}) \;\rightarrow\; \ldots \;\rightarrow\; f_1(\pi_{-i})$$

denoting the set of M increasingly coarser equivalence classifications of the history-state π_{-i}, we linearly interpolate the higher order estimates $p_{\mathrm{ML}}\big(w|f_m(\pi_{-i})\big)$ with lower order estimates $p_{\mathrm{ML}}\big(w|f_{m-1}(\pi_{-i})\big)$ as

$$\begin{aligned} & p_{\mathrm{JM}}(w_i|f_m(\pi_{-i})) \\ &\quad = \lambda_{f_m} p_{\mathrm{ML}}(w_i|f_m(\pi_{-i})) \\ &\qquad +(1-\lambda_{f_m}) p_{\mathrm{JM}}(w_i|f_{m-1}(\pi_{-i})), \end{aligned}$$

for $1 \leq m \leq M$, where the 0-th order model $p_{\mathrm{JM}}(w_i|f_0(\pi_{-i}))$ is a uniform distribution.

The coefficients $\lambda_{f_m(\pi_{-i})}$ are estimated on a held-out set using the bucketing algorithm suggested by Bahl (1983), which ties $\lambda_{f_m(\pi_{-i})}$'s based on the count of $f_m(\pi_{-i})$'s in the training data. We use the expected count of the features from the last iteration of EM training, since the π_{-i} are latent states.

We perform the bucketing algorithm for each level $f_1, f_2, \cdots, f_M$ of equivalence classification separately, and estimate the bucketed $\lambda_{c(f_m)}$ using the Baum-Welch algorithm (Baum, 1972) to maximize the likelihood of held out data, where the word probability assignment in Eq. 1 is replaced with:

$$p(w_i|W_{-i}) = \sum_{j=1}^{|\Pi_i|} p_{\mathrm{JM}}\Big(w_i|f_M(\pi^j_{-i})\Big)\, p_g(\pi^j_{-i}|W_{-i}).$$

The hierarchy shown in Figure 4 is used[1] for obtaining a smooth estimate $p_{\mathrm{JM}}(\cdot|\cdot)$ at each level.

5 SLM Experiments

We train a dependency SLM for two different tasks, namely *Broadcast News* (`BN`) and *Wall Street Journal* (`WSJ`). Unlike Section 3.2, where we swept through multiple training sets of multiple sizes,

[1]The original SLM hierarchical interpolation scheme is aggressive in that it drops both the tag and headword from the history. However, in many cases the headword's tag alone is sufficient, suggesting a more gradual interpolation. Keeping the headtag adds more specific information and at the same time is less sparse. A similar idea is found, e.g., in the back-off hierarchical class n-gram language model (Zitouni, 2007) where instead of backing off from the n-gram right to the $(n-1)$-gram a more gradual backoff — by considering a hierarchy of fine-to-coarse classes for the last word in the history— is used.

training the SLM is computationally intensive. Yet, useful insights may be gained from the $40M$ word case. So we choose the source of text *most suitable* for each task, and proceed as follows.

5.1 Setup

The following summarizes the setup for each task:

- `BN` **setup** : EARS BN03 corpus, which has about $42M$ words serves as our training text. We also use rt04 ($45K$ words) as our evaluation data. Finally, to interpolate our structured language models with the baseline 4-gram model, we use rt03+dev04f (about $40K$ words) data sets to serve as our development set. The vocabulary we use in BN experiments has about $84K$ words.
- `WSJ` **setup** : The training text consists of about $37M$ words. We use eval92+eval93 ($10K$ words) as our evaluation set and dev93 ($9K$ words) serves as our development set for interpolating SLMs with the baseline 4-gram model.

In both cases, we sample about $20K$ sentences from the training text (we exclude them from training data) to serve as our heldout data for applying the bucketing algorithm and estimating λ's. To apply the dependency parser, all the data sets are first converted to Treebank-style tokenization and POS-tagged using the tagger of (Tsuruoka et al., 2011)[2]. Both the POS-tagger and the shift-reduce dependency parser are trained on the Broadcast News treebank from Ontonotes (Weischedel et al., 2008) and the WSJ Penn Treebank (after converting them to dependency trees) which consists of about $1.2M$ tokens. Finally, we train a modified kneser-ney 4-gram LM on the tokenized training text to serve as our baseline LM, for both experiments.

5.2 Results and Analysis

Table 2 shows the perplexity results for `BN` and `WSJ` experiments, respectively. It is evident that the 4-gram baseline for `BN` is stronger than the $40M$ case of Table 1. Yet, the interpolated SLM significantly improves over the 4-gram LM, as it does for `WSJ`.

[2]To make sure we have a proper LM, the POS-tagger and dependency parser only use features from history to tag a word position and produce the dependency structure. All lookahead features used in (Tsuruoka et al., 2011) and (Sagae and Tsujii, 2007) are excluded.

Language Model	Dev	Eval
`BN`		
Kneser-Ney 4-gram	165	158
SLM	168	159
KN+SLM Interpolation	**147**	**142**
`WSJ`		
Kneser-Ney 4-gram	144	121
SLM	149	125
KN+SLM Interpolation	**132**	**110**

Table 2: Test set perplexities for different LMs on the `BN` and `WSJ` tasks.

Also, to show that, in fact, the syntactic dependencies modeled through the SLM parameterization is enhancing predictive power of the LM in the problematic regions, i.e. *syntactically-distant* positions, we calculate the following (log) probability ratio for each position in the test data,

$$\log \frac{p_{\text{KN+SLM}}(w_i|W_{-i})}{p_{\text{KN}}(w_i|W_{-i})}, \tag{2}$$

where $p_{\text{KN+SLM}}$ is the word probability assignment of the interpolated SLM at each position, and $p_{\text{KN}}(w_i)$ is the probability assigned by the baseline 4-gram model. The quantity above measures the improvement (or degradation) gained as a result of using the SLM parameterization[3].

Figures 5(a) and 5(b) illustrate the histogram of the above probability ratio for all the word positions in evaluation data of `BN` and `WSJ` tasks, respectively. In these figures the histograms for *syntactically-distant* and *syntactically-local* are shown separately to measure the effect of the SLM for either of the position types. It can be observed in the figures that for both tasks the percentage of positions with $\log \frac{p_{\text{KN+SLM}}(w_i|W_{-i})}{p_{\text{KN}}(w_i|W_{-i})}$ around zero is much higher for *syntactically-local* (blue bars) than the *syntactically-distant* (red bars). To confirm this, we calculate the average $\log \frac{p_{\text{KN+SLM}}(w_i|W_{-i})}{p_{\text{KN}}(w_i|W_{-i})}$ —this is the average log-likelihood improvement, which is directly

[3]If $\log \frac{p_{\text{KN+SLM}}(w_i|W_{-i})}{p_{\text{KN}}(w_i|W_{-i})}$ is greater than zero, then the SLM has a better predictive power for word position w_i. This is a meaningful comparison due to the fact that the probability assignment using both SLM and n-gram is a proper probability (which sums to one over all words at each position).

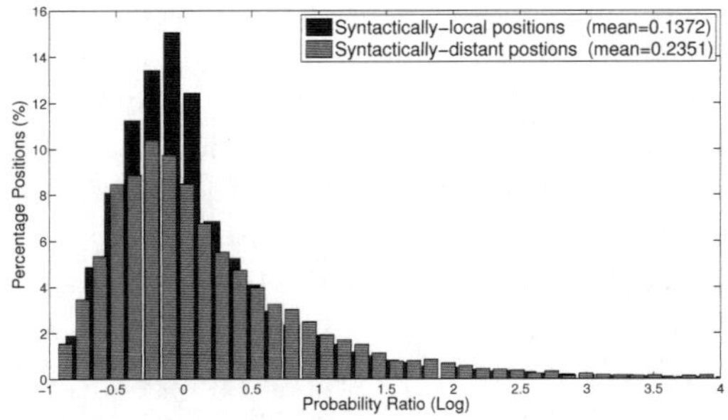

(a) BN

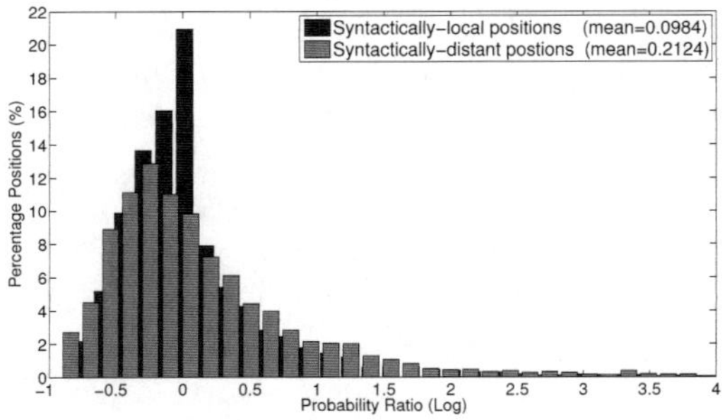

(b) WSJ

Figure 5: Probability ratio histogram of SLM to 4-gram model for (a) BN task (b) WSJ task.

related to perplexity improvement— for each position type in the figures.

Table 3, reports the perplexity performance of each LM (baseline 4-gram, SLM and interpolated SLM) on different positions of the evaluation data for BN and WSJ tasks. As it can be observed from this table, the use of long-span dependencies in the SLM partially fills the gap between the performance of the baseline 4-gram LM on *syntactically-distant* positions $\mathcal{N}$ versus *syntactically-local* positions $\mathcal{M}$. In addition, it can be seen that the SLM by itself fills the gap substantially, however, due to its underlying parameterization which is based on Jelinek-Mercer smoothing it has a worse performance on regular *syntactically-local* positions (which account for the majority of the positions) compared to the Kneser-Ney smoothed LM[4]. Therefore, to improve the overall performance, the interpolated SLM takes advantage of both the better modeling performance of Kneser-Ney for *syntactically-local* positions and the better features included in the SLM for improving predictive power on *syntactically-distant* positions.

[4]This is merely due to the superior modeling power and better smoothing of the Kneser-Ney LM (Chen and Goodman, 1998).

Test Set	4-gram	SLM	4-gram + SLM
Position	BN		
$\mathcal{M}$	146	152	132
$\mathcal{N}$	201	182	171
$\mathcal{N}+\mathcal{M}$	158	159	142
$\frac{PPL_{\mathcal{N}}}{PPL_{\mathcal{M}}}$	138%	120%	129%
	WSJ		
$\mathcal{M}$	114	120	105
$\mathcal{N}$	152	141	131
$\mathcal{N}+\mathcal{M}$	121	125	110
$\frac{PPL_{\mathcal{N}}}{PPL_{\mathcal{M}}}$	133%	117%	125%

Table 3: Perplexity on the BN and WSJ evaluation sets for the 4-gram LM, SLM and their interpolation. The SLM has lower perplexity than the 4-gram in *syntactically distant* positions $\mathcal{N}$, and has a smaller discrepancy $\frac{PPL_{\mathcal{N}}}{PPL_{\mathcal{M}}}$ between preplexity on the distant and local predictions, complementing the 4-gram model.

6 Conclusion

The results of Table 1 and Figure 2 suggest that predicting the next word is about 50% more difficult when its syntactic dependence on the history reaches beyond n-gram range. They also suggest that this difficulty does not diminish with increasing training data size. If anything, the relative difficulty of word positions with nonlocal dependencies relative to those with local dependencies appears to *increase* with increasing training data and n-gram order. Finally, it appears that language models that exploit long-distance syntactic dependencies explicitly at positions where the n-gram is least effective are beneficial as complementary models.

Tables 2 and 3 demonstrates that a particular, recently-proposed SLM with such properties improves a 4-gram LM trained on a large corpus.

Acknowledgments

Thanks to Kenji Sagae for sharing his shift-reduce dependency parser and the anonymous reviewers for helpful comments.

References

LR Bahl. 1983. A maximum likelihood approach to continuous speech recognition. *IEEE Transactions on Pattern Analysis and Machine Inteligence (PAMI)*, 5(2):179–190.

L. E. Baum. 1972. An equality and associated maximization technique in statistical estimation for probabilistic functions of Markov processes. *Inequalities*, 3:1–8.

C. Chelba and F. Jelinek. 2000. Structured language modeling. *Computer Speech and Language*, 14(4):283–332.

SF Chen and J Goodman. 1998. An empirical study of smoothing techniques for language modeling. Technical report, Computer Science Group, Harvard University.

S. Chen, B. Kingsbury, L. Mangu, D. Povey, G. Saon, H. Soltau, and G. Zweig. 2006. Advances in speech transcription at IBM under the DARPA EARS program. *IEEE Transactions on Audio, Speech and Language Processing*, pages 1596–1608.

M Collins, B Roark, and M Saraclar. 2005. Discriminative syntactic language modeling for speech recognition. In *ACL*.

Ahmad Emami and Frederick Jelinek. 2005. A Neural Syntactic Language Model. *Machine learning*, 60:195–227.

Denis Filimonov and Mary Harper. 2009. A joint language model with fine-grain syntactic tags. In *EMNLP*.

John Garofolo, Jonathan Fiscus, William Fisher, and David Pallett, 1996. *CSR-IV HUB4*. Linguistic Data Consortium, Philadelphia.

Zhongqiang Huang and Mary Harper. 2009. Self-Training PCFG grammars with latent annotations across languages. In *EMNLP*.

Frederick Jelinek and Robert L. Mercer. 1980. Interpolated estimation of Markov source parameters from sparse data. In *Proceedings of the Workshop on Pattern Recognition in Practice*, pages 381–397.

S. Khudanpur and J. Wu. 2000. Maximum entropy techniques for exploiting syntactic, semantic and collocational dependencies in language modeling. *Computer Speech and Language*, pages 355–372.

H. K. J. Kuo, L. Mangu, A. Emami, I. Zitouni, and L. Young-Suk. 2009. Syntactic features for Arabic speech recognition. In *Proc. ASRU*.

M.P. Marcus, M.A. Marcinkiewicz, and B. Santorini. 1993. Building a large annotated corpus of English: The Penn Treebank. *Computational Linguistics*, 19(2):330.

Ariya Rastrow, Mark Dredze, and Sanjeev Khudanpur. 2011. Efficient discrimnative training of long-span language models. In *IEEE Workshop on Automatic Speech Recognition and Understanding (ASRU)*.

K. Sagae and J. Tsujii. 2007. Dependency parsing and domain adaptation with LR models and parser ensembles. In *Proc. EMNLP-CoNLL*, volume 7, pages 1044–1050.

Yoshimasa Tsuruoka, Yusuke Miyao, and Jun'ichi Kazama. 2011. Learning with Lookahead : Can History-Based Models Rival Globally Optimized Models ? In *Proc. CoNLL*, number June, pages 238–246.

Ralph Weischedel, Sameer Pradhan, Lance Ramshaw, Martha Palmer, Nianwen Xue, Mitchell Marcus, Ann Taylor, Craig Greenberg, Eduard Hovy, Robert Belvin, and Ann Houston, 2008. *OntoNotes Release 2.0*. Linguistic Data Consortium, Philadelphia.

Imed Zitouni. 2007. Backoff hierarchical class n-gram language models: effectiveness to model unseen events in speech recognition. *Computer Speech & Language*, 21(1):88–104.

Author Index